Comments on other *Ama~...~* ....

"*Tightly written volumes filled with lots of wit and humour about famous and infamous Canadians.*"
Eric Shackleton, *The Globe and Mail*

"*The heightened sense of drama and intrigue, combined with a good dose of human interest is what sets* Amazing Stories *apart.*"
Pamela Klaffke, *Calgary Herald*

"*This is popular history as it should be...For this price, buy two and give one to a friend.*"
Terry Cook, a reader from Ottawa, on **Rebel Women**

"*Glasner creates the moment of the explosion itself in graphic detail...she builds detail upon gruesome detail to create a convincingly authentic picture.*"
Peggy McKinnon, *The Sunday Herald,* on **The Halifax Explosion**

"*It was wonderful...I found I could not put it down. I was sorry when it was completed.*"
Dorothy F. from Manitoba on **Marie-Anne Lagimodière**

"*Stories are rich in description, and bristle with a clever, stylish realness.*"
Mark Weber, *Central Alberta Advisor,* on **Ghost Town Stories II**

"*A compelling read. Bertin...has selected only the most intriguing tales, which she narrates with a wealth of detail.*"
Joyce Glasner, *New Brunswick Reader,* on **Strange Events**

"*The resulting book is one readers will want to share with all the women in their lives.*"
Lynn Martel, *Rocky Mountain Outlook,* on **Women Explorers**

MAURICE RICHARD

The Most Amazing Hockey Player Ever

Chris Robinson

SPORTS HISTORY

James Lorimer & Company Ltd., Publishers
Toronto

James Lorimer & Company Ltd., Publishers acknowledge the support of the Ontario Arts Council. We acknowledge the financial support of the Government of Canada through the Canada Book Fund for our publishing activities. We acknowledge the support of the Canada Council for the Arts which last year invested $20.1 million in writing and publishing throughout Canada. We acknowledge the support of the Government of Ontario through the Ontario Media Development Corporation's Ontario Book Initiative.

Canada Council
for the Arts

ONTARIO ARTS COUNCIL
CONSEIL DES ARTS DE L'ONTARIO

Library and Archives Canada Cataloguing in Publication

Robinson, Chris, 1967-
Maurice Richard : the most amazing hockey player ever / Chris
Robinson.

(Amazing stories)
Includes bibliographical references and index.
Issued also in electronic format.
ISBN 978-1-55277-900-2

1. Richard, Maurice, 1921-2000. 2. Hockey players--Québec
(Province)--Biography. I. Title. II. Series: Amazing stories (Toronto, Ont.)

GV848.5.R5R62 2011   796.962092   C2011-904529-X

James Lorimer & Company Ltd., Publishers
317 Adelaide Street West, Suite 1002
Toronto, ON, Canada
M5V 1P9
www.lorimer.ca

Printed in Canada

FSC
www.fsc.org
MIX
Paper from
responsible sources
FSC® C016245

For my sons,
Harrison and Jarvis

Contents

Prologue

Monday, March 11th 1996

The Montreal Canadiens had just defeated the Dallas Stars 4–1. It's wasn't a particularly memorable game, but that night was not about the game. Fans across Canada had gathered to bid farewell to the great shrine and its ghosts, thrills, disappointments, and championships. The Forum has been viewed by many as the cathedral of Quebec, a place where French-Canadians gathered and celebrated a common past, one led by their deity, Maurice "Rocket" Richard.

During the post-game ceremony, former Canadiens stars were welcomed to the red carpets at centre ice. Guy Lafleur, Frank Mahovlich, Ken Dryden, Jean Béliveau, Elmer Lach, Yvan Cournoyer, Lorne "Gump" Worsley, and Henri Richard are among those introduced to the roaring Forum crowd.

Then came the Rocket. The man, the player they had been waiting for.

As the Rocket walked to centre ice, the evening transformed into something spiritual, a celebration and farewell to the man who inspired a riot in the streets of Montreal; who with fire, passion, determination, and a wooden stick, injected the oppressed and fragile people of Quebec with hope and confidence. For a chilling and emotional eight minutes, the Forum faithful stood to honour Richard, a man who was more than a hockey player. He was a hero.

Throughout the Forum, people applauded through tears. The usually reserved Rocket, who always insisted that he was just a hockey player, stood teary eyed and seemingly embarrassed.

"I was just a hockey player," he thought. "Just a human being like everyone else."

He waved his hands in an attempt to quiet the crowd. This was one battle he lost. His worshippers would not be silenced.

In these final moments, Richard inspired an entire country to come together as one.

For one evening, we were all Rocket Richards.

Chapter 1
The Montreal Canadiens

Before the Rocket came the Montreal Canadiens. Yet, conversely, without the Rocket, the Canadiens might have vanished into the history books.

To better understand the life, career, and cultural impact on Quebec culture and English–French-Canadian relations, it's necessary to put Richard's legacy in the context of the Montreal Canadiens history.

Thanks in large part to Richard, "in the history of Quebec, there have been two great institutions, the Catholic Church and the Montreal Canadiens. Religion would like to be like the Canadiens. The Church has lost some prestige, but the

Canadiens are an institution."

Strangely enough, the team that had come to represent French-Canadians was founded by two English-speaking businessmen.

In 1909, the National Hockey Association was made up of English Canadian teams (Renfrew, Ottawa, Cobalt, Haileybury, and Montreal) and rich English-Canadian owners. Two of those owners, Jimmy Gardner, owner of the Montreal Wanderers (which primarily appealed to English Montrealers), and Ambrose O'Brien, believed that forming a French team in Montreal would be a financial boon to their hockey franchises and the league in general. A French team would also provide a rivalry for the Wanderers and ideally attract the interest and cash of the French-Canadian population. Under the guidance of O'Brien, the Club de Hockey Canadien was born.

Although the team was given first rights to French-Canadian players—notably star players Dietre Pietre and Newsy Lalonde, who won the scoring championship in the Canadiens' inaugural year—it failed to capture the attention of French-Canadians. "The Canadiens," wrote Tancrède Marsil of *Le Devoir*, "only represent the interests and the money of Mr. O'Brien and not our French-Canadian nationality."

To the joy of Marsil and other French Montrealers, O'Brien's stay was short-lived. In October 1910, George Kennedy, the owner of the French-speaking sports club Club Athlétique Canadien, threatened to sue the Canadiens for

Franchise saviour.

A joyful Rocket takes hold of the Stanley Cup.

infringing on their name. Kennedy told the NHA that if he wasn't given a franchise, he would take the matter to court.

The shrewd O'Brien saw no point in going to court over the matter. He figured that the members of Kennedy's club would very likely become devoted hockey fans. Kennedy was given ownership of the Club de Hockey Canadien.

Led by Pietre, Lalonde, and goaltender Georges Vezina, the Canadiens rose up the standings and quickly captured the imagination of French-Canadians. Fans lined up to see their new team. Local newspapers began celebrating each victory. One paper wrote: "For a culture humbled by Montreal's Anglo-Scots business crowd and subdued by their own Catholic heritage, the Canadiens were a chance for French-Canadians to celebrate vicariously."

Anticipating decades of political and cultural rollercoaster rides between the Canadiens and the French-Canadian press, Marsil blasted Kennedy in *Le Devoir* for signing an Irish-Canadian player, James Power. The signing, for Marsil, was "polluting the character of the Canadiens and creating a deplorable and ill-advised precedent by allowing Anglo-Saxon blood to infiltrate this club which we are proud to call our own."

Marsil didn't seem to notice that although Newsy Lalonde had a French name, he couldn't speak French. Power, on the other hand—despite his English name—spoke perfect French.

Under Kennedy's guidance, the Canadiens won three league titles and a Stanley Cup in 1916. However, things would not remain so rosy. The 1919 Stanley Cup final between the Canadiens and the Seattle Metropolitans was cancelled because of the Spanish flu epidemic which had affected players from both teams. Montreal player Big Joe Hall died four days after the series was cancelled. Kennedy would die two years later; he never fully recovered from the effects of the flu.

After Kennedy's death, the Canadiens were purchased by three men, led by Leo Dandurand, a French-speaking American. Carrying on Kennedy's success, Dandurand quickly assembled a formidable roster led by the great Howie Morenz.

Long before Richard, Howe, Gretzky, and Crosby, there was Morenz. His dazzling skills and blistering speed captured not only the imagination of French- and English-Canadians, but also those of fans throughout the NHL. In fact, Morenz's seat-lifting plays led the creation of two American teams: the Boston Bruins and the New York Americans.

Morenz filled stadiums. Playing on a line with Aurèle Joliat, the duo led the Canadiens to three Stanley Cups between 1924 and 1931.

But in 1934, with Morenz entering the twilight of his career, the Canadiens traded him. Losing their superstar proved to have devastating results. With the Depression crippling the city, box office sales had plummeted. Cheap tickets

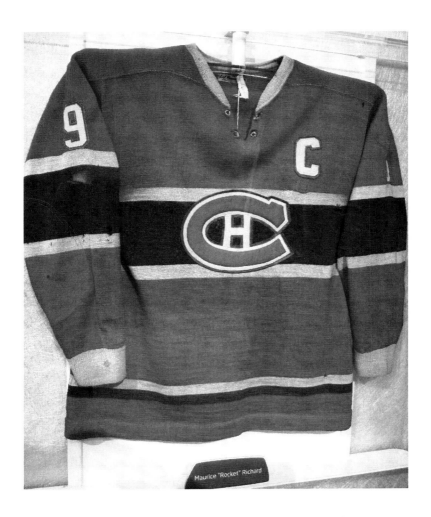

Two legends are born: Rocket Richard and the Montreal Canadiens.

were no longer affordable. And the team was suffering on the ice without Morenz. The team wasn't making money. They were in such a sorry state that the franchise came close to being moved to Cleveland.

Desperate for a spark, the Canadiens reacquired Morenz in September 1936. A rejuvenated Morenz was on his way to his best season in years...and then tragedy struck. During a game on January 28, 1937, Morenz slid into the end boards. His leg snapped in four places. Six weeks later, he died. Myths abounded over the cause of death. Joliat, his friend and team-mate, said that Morenz had died of a broken heart. While that sums up the essence of the tragedy, the truth is more complicated. Fearing he would never play again, Morenz drank heavily in the hospital and eventually had a heart attack.

On March 11, 1937, a funeral was held for Morenz at the Forum. Hundreds of people lined up for hours to bid farewell to their hero.

The Canadiens chose to honour Morenz by retiring his jersey number, 7 (they were the first team to retire a player's number), and hosting a benefit all-star game for his family. At the time of his death, Morenz held the NHL record for career points with 472. He was among the first players inducted into the Hockey Hall of Fame and was viewed by many as the greatest hockey player of the time.

In another irony of the Canadiens' history, Morenz, worshipped by English- and French-Canadians, was born in

Ontario and spoke no French. What must have Marsil thought of an English-Canadian being hailed as a hero by French-Canadians!

The death of Morenz sent the Canadiens into a tailspin that lasted until the mid-1940s. With the retirement of the devastated Joliat, the team sank to the bottom of the standings. With a primarily English-Canadian roster, French-Canadians no longer felt a connection to the team.

"By the time the Second World War broke out," wrote Roch Carrier, "the Canadiens were a sorry franchise, existing on loans and charity from other NHL clubs. Their financial and hockey resources were at a low ebb and it seemed their every move was wrong."

Like other Canadians, Quebecers had suffered through a severe economic depression that only ended when World War II erupted. The war was not popular in Quebec, with many feeling that this was Europe's war and that Canada had no business fighting in it. When Prime Minister Mackenzie King's conscription law passed, tensions between English and French Canada heightened. For the French, this was yet another example of the arrogant English dictating their lives. To make matters worse, Quebec was entering "The Great Blackness" under the control of the strongly conservative Maurice Duplessis. During his eventual eighteen years as premier (starting in 1936), Duplessis's paranoid, intolerant policies turned Quebec into an impoverished, almost backwater state.

After decades of church, state, and English oppression, Quebec was on the edge of eruption. French-Canadians needed hope.

No one could have imagined that hope would come in the form of a hockey player.

Chapter 2
Rocket Launch

Onésime Richard lived in the Gaspé Peninsula on the shores of the St. Lawrence River. Prospects were dim for the people of the area. The soil was rocky. The winters were brutally cold. Houses were crammed with undernourished people.

In a description that could equally define Maurice Richard, writer Charles Foran wrote that "Gaspesians were known for their pride, stubbornness, and hard work, and though isolated by language, most had grown up in the company of equally working-class Anglophones along the New Brunswick border."

One day Onésime decided that he had seen enough.

A proud and independent man, Onésime packed up and left for Montreal, where he hoped that his modest training as a carpenter would land him work.

English Montrealers lived primarily in Westmount and Notre-Dame-de-Grâce on the west side of Montreal, while the French majority resided on the east side of the city. Foran noted, "Some seven hundred thousand people called the island of Montreal home in 1921, rending it a distinctly New World urban stew of languages and identities."

During a social event for homesick exiles, the quiet, brooding Onésime met another Gaspé native, Alice Laramée. They fell in love and, in this new environment of hope and relative prosperity, married in October 1920.

Shortly after, on August 4, 1921, Alice delivered a baby boy who would go on to inspire hope, passion, and confidence in future generations of French-Canadians: Maurice Richard.

Maurice Richard was born during a time of turmoil throughout Canada and Quebec. Three years after World War I, people were struggling to find work. Rural Quebec, in particular, was hit hard.

The newly married couple settled in the east end of the city near Lafontaine Park. Onésime found odd jobs as a carpenter and then as a woodworker for the Canadian Pacific Railway. The work was ideal for Onésime, as he had security and benefits and was close to the family's new home in the

Bordeaux village, just north of downtown Montreal.

Onésime worried that his dream wouldn't last. The unemployment rate had soared throughout Quebec and Canada. But he found a distraction. In 1924, the Montreal Canadiens won the Stanley Cup. And they won it again in 1929. Onésime, like many Québécois, burst with joy and a newfound confidence. Despite the economical and political turmoil around them, French-Canadians embraced the team. When the Canadiens won, the people of Quebec won.

Onésime had already decided that Maurice would play hockey. He had bought Maurice skates when he was just four years old. Maurice put them on and never took them off. He played with bigger boys and learned how to skate as fast as they could and hit as hard as they did.

Living his life on the ice, Richard had no idea of the turmoil taking place around him. The federal government had taken Labrador from Quebec. Anglo businesses dominated Montreal. Owners paid French-Canadians a quarter of what their Anglophone neighbours earned. Many French-Canadian families lived below the threshold of poverty.

Quebec also wondered why they received less financial aid than the rest of the provinces. French-Canadians were fed up with Anglos pushing them around. Immigrants were taking jobs. Communist and socialist groups emerged, calling for a revolution.

Montreal mayor Camillien Houde created jobs through

Maurice Richard

The fiery eyes that would haunt many NHL goalies for years to come.

a variety of initiatives. Highways, tunnels, playgrounds, and shelters were built. Yet Houde's valiant attempts did little to improve the economic situation.

By 1929, local businesses were collapsing. The unemployment rate reached 31 per cent. Lacking funds, universities and schools were forced to close. Families were evicted, their furniture smothering the streets. Men spent their days lined up outside factories with the hope of finding work. Soup kitchens were overwhelmed and the Church put up shelters for those who'd lost their homes.

And then Onésime's years of worry finally manifested. In 1930, he lost his job. Barely able to support his eight children *with* a job, how could he provide for them with no money? The family was forced to take food coupons through the government's direct assistance initiative. Onésime was embarrassed. Maurice would go to the grocer's with the coupons. Nine-year-old Maurice ran errands and briefly took a job as a caddy at a local golf course.

But when Maurice took to the ice, he lived in another world void of misery and suffering. And each time he laced up those skates, he shaped his destiny. Roch Carrier once noted, "Every time he gets hold of the puck, Maurice starts a new life. The one he was given is of no importance. He grabs the puck and invents his life."

Growing up in the heavily French-Canadian area of Bordeaux, the Richard family continued to expand. Maurice couldn't stand the noise. The home was crowded; a baby was always crying. So he found refuge outdoors. Maurice and his friends skated on the river, on public rinks, and on the backyard rink that his father built. Winters were so cold that Maurice and his friends even skated on the streets to school.

Onésime's passion for the Canadiens passed down to Maurice. He began listening to radio broadcasts of Canadiens games every Saturday night. His father told him of the team's past stars, Aurèle Joliat and, of course, the great Howie Morenz, whose flashy, determined style made him the darling of Canadiens' fans.

Yet amid the joys of listening to the Canadiens' play, just outside the Richards' doors was a world of turmoil. Throughout the province, some called for separation from Canada. "We will have our French state," historian Abbé Lionel Groulx tells thousands of French-Canadians who gathered to listen at a French-language congress. "And we will have a French country, a country that will carry its soul on its face."

Many in Quebec scream their approval. Others are not so keen, including Premier Maurice Duplessis.

"The world doesn't offer much hope to French-Canadians," wrote Roch Carrier in his book, *Our Life with the Rocket*. "It is on the verge of giving birth to a storm. You can feel it coming...We value our religion. We value our French language...the language that the English masters tried to make us forget."

Rocket Launch

Richard—not a politician or a priest, but a hockey player
—was that brewing storm that Carrier predicted.

* * *

Maurice listened to his father's Canadiens' lore, but only
cared about the current players, specifically Hector "Toe"
Blake. During radio broadcasts, he would close his eyes and
imagine being at the Forum, hearing the explosive roar of the
fans, watching Blake skate toward the net, firing the puck.
"Hearing the announcer say 'Blake shoots, he scores!' was the
greatest thrill I could have in those days," Richard wrote years
later.

The young Richard desperately wanted to see his beloved Canadiens play at the Forum. But the cost of a ticket and
streetcar ride was too pricey for Richard and his family. The
Forum was also located on the predominantly English west
end of Montreal. Unable to speak English, Richard was wary
about leaving his neighbourhood and entering this alien
world.

Beyond money, there was also the issue of time. Richard
spent his free time playing and dreaming hockey. By grade
nine, Richard had played peewee, midget, and bantam hockey. The game he loved most though was called 'hog.' A player
would take the puck and try to keep it away from everyone.

Hog played an important role in Richard's development, improving his strength, speed, reflexes, and stickhandling abilities.

After graduating from high school, Richard enrolled in the Montreal Technical School and played for their hockey team. He also played for the Bordeaux district team, where he met fellow Montrealer Paul Stuart.

Stuart was in charge of fourteen rinks in the Park Lafontaine area, and he did his best to encourage French-Canadian players. Stuart saw something special in Richard and took him under his wing. But Stuart immediately saw that Richard needed to be tougher to make the NHL. He had Richard take boxing lessons with a local prizefighter, a skill that would prove helpful in his future. Stuart tried, to no avail, to get the still predominately Anglo Canadiens attention.

One day, through Stuart, Montreal businessman Paul-Emile Paquette sees Richard play and offers him a contract to join the Parc Lafontaine juvenile league. In Richard's eyes, that was the pros. The team travelled to games in Paquette's panelled truck and even had a doctor on hand to provide free medical care.

When Richard first took to the ice, he didn't disappoint.

In his first game, he scored six goals. He soon led the team to three straight juvenile championships.

"In 1938–1939," Paquette said later, "our team played forty-six games, winning forty-three, tying two, and losing only one. The team scored 144 goals and Maurice scored 133 of these. We were in a habit of winning games 10–0 and 12–0, and Richard was getting eight or ten goals by himself. We counted on him to provided three-quarters of our offence."

It was during this time that Richard met Lucille Norchet, the sister of his friend, Georges. The two were smitten with each other from the start. They eventually married in 1942 and would go on to spend the rest of their lives together. Lucille would prove to be a guiding light in Richard's life, frequently reassuring, supporting, and protecting him. Meanwhile, hockey people began noticing Richard. With no formal scouting system in place, the attention didn't mean much. "They owned four or five junior teams and controlled senior hockey too, but it was run like a bad orchard," recalled Richard. "They waited until the wind would blow apples out of the trees.

"If you were any good," Richard continued, "you would eventually work your way up and they would notice you. It was nothing like today's junior leagues..."

The Canadiens didn't have territorial rights to Quebec players, so Richard could have been signed by any NHL team; however, none of the other NHL teams generally pursued Montreal players, giving the Canadiens free reign over Quebec hockey.

Following his incredible season with the Paquette team, Richard was invited to try out for the Junior A Verdun Maple

Leafs. Along with 126 players, Richard attended the Leafs' 1939 training camp with high hopes. "Just being invited to camp at that level meant something special," said Richard. He made the team, but spent a fair bit of time on the bench or playing on the third and fourth lines. And, although players weren't allowed to play for multiple teams, Richard found playing time with the Paquette team, using the pseudonym Maurice Rochon.

As the season went on, Richard played more and gained confidence. Soon, he was on the first line. Come playoff time, Richard, anticipating his clutch scoring with the Canadiens, came to life, scoring seven goals and sixteen points during the team's seven playoff games.

Hockey scouts were still unsure if Richard had the makings of an NHL player. Nevertheless, Richard's playoff success caught the eyes of the Montreal Canadiens Seniors—a farm team for the parent NHL Canadiens. He was invited to camp and made the team.

During his first game, the nineteen-year-old Richard flew all over the ice. He scored two goals and was headed for a hat trick. He grabbed the puck and soared down the ice, avoiding and bouncing off opponent's checks. Finally, he was alone. Rocketing toward the net, Richard was suddenly hauled down on a breakaway. He fell and slid uncontrollably, smashing into the boards. He hears a crack in his leg. A broken ankle. His season was over before he even finished his first game.

Rocket Launch

Richard was miserable. Would his leg ever be the same again? Could he still make it as a hockey player? At least he could still work as a machinist. In fact, most of his time had been spent working during the days and playing hockey at night. Being laid up with little to do depressed and frustrated Richard. Fortunately, Lucille was there. She continually reassured him that everything would work out, that he was a hockey player because he was so talented and passionate. Spurred on by Lucille's confidence, Maurice worked hard to strengthen his leg. He promised himself that he would play again.

Lucille's support proved pivotal. Richard returned to hockey in March, just two months after his injury. He was able to play the final game of the regular season and all six playoff games.

Meanwhile, Maurice Rochon scored fifteen of Paquette's seventeen playoff goals.

During the summer of 1941, Richard was called to a recruitment centre. The world was at war, and Richard was proud to be called. Other men his age were dying for their country while he was chasing a black rubber disc on frozen water. In his mind, he believed they were the heroes. He was just playing a trivial game. Richard hoped that he would be able to join the Royal Canadian Air Force.

Despite his desire to serve, Richard was declared unfit for service because of his broken ankle.

Maurice Richard

The following season, Richard returned to the Senior Canadiens fully healed. He manages to play thirty games until January 1941, when another devastating injury occurs. Coming out from behind the opponent's net, Richard fires a backhand at the goalie. As he does, a defencemen slashes him on the leg, knocking Richard off balance. Using his wrist, Richard desperately reaches out to the net to stop his fall. He hears a loud crack. His wrist has hit the metal goalpost and snapped.

Yet again, Richard is forced to sit. People are beginning to doubt Richard. He is too brittle, they whisper. Having broken an ankle and wrist means the end for him.

He sits, immobile and even more frustrated. He can't play hockey. He can't work. He can't go to war. There is nothing to do but heal.

Weeks later, Richard surprises everyone by returning to the ice. He joins the Senior Canadiens for the 1941–42 play-offs and scores six goals in four games.

Richard's increasing success is largely due to his Seniors' coach, Paul Haynes. Haynes felt that the right-shooting Richard would benefit from playing on the left side:

> *A left-handed shooter coming in on the left wing usually has one of two choices if he decides to get in close. One is to try to swing around the left side of the defence, in which*

case he often gets ridden off a good shooting angle by the defencemen on that side and is forced to keep going around the net or to pass back. The other choice is to veer into the heavily populated area in front of the net, which leaves the puck swinging around in front of him into position for a backhand shot.

When, on occasion, he'd find himself way over on the wrong side, he'd button-hook around the other defenceman, using the sheer strength of his left arm, and follow with a burst of speed in between the defenceman and the goal. Normally that would leave a player a prime target to get reefed in the narrow passage by the first defenceman, now out in front of the goal. But so great was the surge of speed that frequently he was out in front before either of the two defencemen or the goalie, realized what was happening. And when Richard pulled the trick, he ended in supreme shooting position as a left-handed shot.

The shift forced other players to develop their backhand shots as well. But Richard possessed one of the best backhands in the NHL. And a great backhand shot is one of the most difficult shots for a goalie to stop.

Then, one day, the Canadiens called on Richard.

Surprisingly, Richard's average seasons with the Leafs and Seniors didn't deter the Montreal Canadiens. "He was playing in Junior A hockey for the Verdun Maple Leafs when I was acting manager of Maple Leaf Gardens," said Frank Selke, who would eventually take over as manager of the Canadiens. "Verdun met Oshawa in the Eastern Canada Memorial Cup semifinals. No one would suspect that the hard-driving Richard would some day rewrite the record book. Richard advanced in hockey under conditions that would have cooled off any less dedicated player."

Richard concurred: "I still can't figure out what they saw in me to offer me that first pro contract. I was hopelessly awkward and fragile. It seemed I was always on my ass or in the hospital."

Hopeless or not, the Rocket was ready to launch.

Chapter 3
Franchise Saviour

When Richard attended his first Canadiens training camp in 1942, he was joining a team in disarray. Once a powerhouse, the Canadiens had not won a Stanley Cup since 1931. The team frequently played in front of empty seats. "When I was playing senior hockey," Richard recalled. "Quite often we would fill the Forum, while the Canadiens played to a half-full Forum. Most of that was because they had been such a bad hockey team for so long. But a large part was because they had few recognizable French-Canadian stars."

In 1927, there were ten teams in the NHL. By 1940, only seven remained. Worried that the Canadiens were about to fold and leave the NHL with six teams, Leafs owner Conn Smythe suggested that his coach, Dick Irvin—who had led the Leafs to three straight Stanley Cup finals—take over the coaching reins in Montreal. If anyone would be able to turn the Canadiens around, Smythe figured, it would be Irvin.

The lack of French-Canadian players was a big problem for the Canadiens. The coach and manager were English. The brightest players came from out west. When Richard joined the Canadiens, the only other French-Canadian players were Butch Bouchard and Fernand Majeau.

The Canadiens felt that there was something special about Richard. He was their best French-Canadian prospect in many years, a natural goal-scorer with the speed and explosiveness of the great Howie Morenz. Irvin and manager Tommy Gorman hoped that the young Richard would become their long sought after French superstar, someone who would fill the Forum again and inspire young French-Canadians to dream of following him to the Montreal Canadiens.

The predominantly English-speaking Canadiens would give Richard new challenges. Unable to speak English, Richard found it difficult to communicate with his Anglo teammates. Richard was not against learning English, but he lived on the French side of Montreal, where people didn't feel they needed to learn English. Richard said that his reputation as a silent, sombre type was misguided. "I was deathly afraid to even try to say anything in English. I'd just sit there silently. It was more shyness than anything else. I knew many English-speaking players from Montreal who lived in Montreal all their lives and can't speak a word of French. At least most French-Canadians would try to speak English."

Still, Richard had no problems with his teammates. "Apart from winning a lot of hockey games," Richard wrote in 1971, "we had a lot of fun on that team." During the season, they would frequently have parties at a player's house or go out on the town. In the off-season, they would play softball together.

But the war was raging. The government insisted that no player could use hockey as a reason for not joining the service. Approximately eighty NHL players had joined the effort. With fewer players, teams reduced their benches to fourteen players. Owing to wartime restrictions on trains, overtime periods were put aside. The government had suggested that the NHL consider suspending play until after the war, but NHL officials convinced them that hockey was good for morale, giving people a momentary escape from economic worries and war.

The shortage of players made Richard's transition to the NHL easier. He knew that he had arrived at the perfect time. "In one sense I was lucky. The war was in full swing and many of the regular Canadiens players had gone off to the armed forces."

The league was desperate for players. The Boston Bruins even signed a sixteen-year-old, Bep Guidolin, the youngest player ever to play in the NHL. The Red Wings signed Harry Lumley, a seventeen-year-old goalie. Retired stars like Auréle Joliat were approached to take jobs as referees.

Richard arrived at camp with a reputation for being fragile. So Irvin sent forward Murph Chamberlain to see if that was indeed the case. During a play he smashed Richard into the boards, knocking him to the ice. A furious Richard got up and went right after Chamberlain. It took a few teammates to save Chamberlain from the grasp of the rookie.

Richard made the team. Both Gorman and Irvin deemed Richard a "natural." On October 29th, 1942, at twenty-one years old, he signed his first contract. He would be a teammate of his hero Toe Blake! Freshly married, 1942 was a glorious year for the new *Habitant*.

His NHL career began well. After his first fifteen games, Richard had a decent five goals and six assists. Was this good enough to be the next Morenz? People argued the question all season. One thing they did agree on was that Richard scored the most unbelievable goals they'd ever seen.

But then things took a familiar turn for the worst during game sixteen against the Boston Bruins. Richard was on the ice for three minutes and was exhausted. Before he could get off ice, the puck headed his way. Richard grabbed it and rushed toward the Boston end. Along the way, Bruins defenceman Jack Crawford greeted Richard with a devastating hit. The impact caused Crawford to tumble on top of

Richard. Richard's leg twisted awkwardly and his ankle was broken once more.

His season was over, and maybe even his career. His chance of becoming the next Morenz was becoming a distant dream.

Sports reporters and fans criticized the Canadiens for signing Richard. They called him a waste of money, a lemon. And Gorman only added fuel to the fire when he told reporters that Maurice Richard was too brittle-boned; his name was being removed from the Canadiens' reserve list.

At that point, any team in the league had a chance to grab Richard. But none of them did. And Irvin felt the team shouldn't give up so fast on Richard. Gorman put Richard back on the Habs' reserve list...although that didn't stop Gorman from trying to unload Richard on the Detroit Red Wings and New York Rangers. Neither team was interested in the talented but seemingly fragile player.

Richard was furious with management practices. "What bothers me most," he said, "was that nobody would come up to you and talk about such things, man-to-man." Gorman wouldn't talk to Richard about their concerns about his fragility, but he never hesitated to bring it up in the papers. Richard's bitterness toward the Canadiens would linger and grow, well after his retirement.

Richard admitted that he was worried about whether or not he would last in the NHL: "Three major injuries in three years—I wondered, too. I knew I was a lot stronger than they gave me credit for; that I could play against anybody in the league. But I was going to have to prove it. It is hard to fight against the other teams and your own coaches, management, and teammates. Getting a reputation that you are injury-prone is something very hard to get rid of. I also knew that if I hurt myself again in the next season or two, the Canadiens might ship me just about anywhere."

Richard returned to training camp in 1943 with many doubts about his future as a hockey player. But once he stepped onto the ice, the doubting voices were silenced. He went all-out during training camp and showed a newfound confidence that his teammates and coaches hadn't seen before. His speed and power were so impressive that it earned him a nickname.

There are endless stories about how Richard got his famous moniker. But Richard tells the story best: "I got the nickname from three players—all at once. It happened in practice. Toe, Elmer, and myself would infuriate the other guys with the way we'd score goals. We used to go around the line of Murph Chamberlain, Ray Getliffe, and Phil Watson so fast that they were amazed at our speed. One day, when I got up a full head of steam, one of them said, 'Watch out! Here comes the Rocket!'"

Reporters at the practice overheard Chamberlain, Getliffe, and Watson shouting "the Rocket" at Richard. The next day, the nickname was in the papers, where it would stay for the rest of his life.

In October that year, Richard and Lucille welcome a baby girl, Huguette. The mighty Richard is reduced to tears by this miracle. He felt as though he'd just won the Stanley Cup. Richard was so moved by the birth that he rushed to see Dick Irvin to tell him that he would wear number nine (he had been wearing number fifteen) in honour of his daughter, who arrived in the world weighing nine pounds. Irvin, surprised by Richard's sensitive side, agreed.

As Roch Carrier wrote: "Number nine: a new life. This simple symbol lies deep inside Maurice's soul, expressing his love for the child and for the mother, his generosity, his paternal instinct, his devotion. This number nine says what he can't say with words."

With this new number and name, The Rocket is born.

On December 30, 1943, Dick Irvin put Richard on a line with Elmer Lach and his hero, Toe Blake. The line clicked immediately. During an 8–3 pasting of the Detroit Red Wings, Richard scores his first hat trick and adds two assists. The newly minted "Punch Line" would lead the Canadiens for the next decade.

Richard finished the 1943–44 season with thirty-two goals and twenty-two assists in forty-six games. The Rocket then exploded in the playoffs with an NHL record twelve tallies. Most famously, during the first round of the playoffs against Toronto, Richard scored all five of the Canadiens' goals and was named all three stars of the game.

During game one of the finals against Chicago, the Rocket scored all three goals in a 3–1 victory. They won two more games to go up 3–0 in the series. But midway through the final period of game four, the Canadiens found themselves down 4–1. The Habs were playing sloppy hockey without focus and drive. They looked lost, and the fans were restless. After all, the team's last Stanley Cup came in 1931 during the Depression and fans had been waiting thirteen years for another Cup. How on earth could the Canadiens be losing to the inferior Black Hawks?

Some fans began to think that the Canadiens were intentionally losing. The longer the series went on, the more money the players earned. "Fake! Fake! Fake!" the angry fans screamed.

Perhaps motivated by the accusation, the Punch Line came to life with just five minutes left in the game. First, Elmer Lach fires a sizzling shot past goalie Mike Karakas.

4–2.

With the few minutes left in the game ticking away, the Rocket fires an explosive backhand shot past Karakas. They were only one goal behind now. Would it be possible? The fans believed. The team believed.

Less than a minute later, Toe Blake carries the puck behind the Hawks' net. Unable to find an opening, he passes

Rocket, Elmer Lach, and Toe Blake: the powerful Punch Line.

the puck through the legs of the Chicago defenders to the Rocket, who pounds the puck past Karakas.

4–4. Overtime.

The shouts of "fake" had been vanquished.

The Habs came flying out for overtime. They dominated, but the Hawks put up a strong defence and frustrated the Habs' assault—until the ninth minute. From the blue line, Butch Bouchard rifled a pass to Blake, who fired the puck into the net.

After thirteen long years, the Canadiens had won the

Stanley Cup! The city came alive, the war briefly forgotten. Celebrations raged throughout the streets of Montreal, and the city heralded their new hero. Over a thousand people attended a tribute to the Rocket, showering him with praise and gifts. Hope and joy wound its way through a city rife with economic, political, and language conflicts. Richard had captured the hearts of French-Canadians. And they returned to the Forum in droves. The Rocket, the Habs, and the Forum provided solace, a sanctuary where French-Canadians sat, hoped, and dreamed as one.

Feeding off their Cup victory, the Canadiens lost only eight games during the 1944–45 season. Not everyone was impressed with the team or Richard, however. "He's just a wartime hockey player," sportswriters declared. In their opinion, the Habs were little more than a wartime powerhouse playing in a watered down league against weakened opponents. Critics refused to give the Canadiens and the Punch Line (who finished 1-2-3 in points in the NHL that season) any credit. They argued that once the war ended and players returned, the team would return to being average.

There was a whisper of truth to the complaints. Several of the NHL's top players *had* joined the war: the entire "Kraut Line" of the Bruins had gone; the Rangers had also lost an entire line; and the Leafs were without Turk Broda and Syl Apps, two of their best players. (It is true that the Punch Line never reached the same success during this post-war era.)

Franchise Saviour

One sportswriter came to Richard's defence. Elmer Ferguson wrote, "We all know about goals being cheaper this wartime season and the quality of hockey deteriorated, but this is still the major league of hockey and 32 goals in 30 games is a remarkable feat."

Later on, when the Canadiens continued to remain near the top of the NHL standings during the post-war years, Dick Irvin would sharply remind those same critics that, "Yes, there was a war, and it must still be going on if what you guys said was true."

But at that moment, Richard didn't care what the critics said. He now knew he belonged in the NHL. And he would prove it on December 28th, 1944 in a game against the Detroit Red Wings. "The night before," recalled Richard, "I had moved my family to another house. I think I slept two or three hours during the night. I went to Dick and told him that I wasn't feeling very good, and if he wanted to put somebody in my place I would be glad to rest. He said, 'Oh no. You get dressed and see how it's gonna go.'"

And boy did he go. By the final whistle, Richard had set a single game NHL record with five goals and three assists.

By January 1945, the Rocket was scoring at a record pace. After thirty games, he'd scored thirty-two goals. The NHL record was forty-four, set in 1917–18 by former Hab Joe Malone.

But it wasn't just the goals that brought fans out of their seats, it was the way the Rocket scored them.

45

Maurice Richard

One of the most memorable goals in hockey history came during a game against Detroit. Rocketing past the Wings' blue line, Richard headed to the net. Greeting him was Detroit's rough and tumble defenceman, Earl Siebert. Richard saw him, lowered his head, and carried on toward the net. Seibert moved toward the speeding Rocket. The two collided but stayed on their skates. Richard still had the puck. Seibert grabbed hold of Richard and Richard tried to shake him off, but to no avail. The Rocket was determined. Carrying Seibert on his back now, each push of Richard's blades cut into the ice. Regaining speed, Richard moved the puck and Seibert toward the net. Seibert tried to dig his blades into the ice to stop Richard, but it was no use. Richard skated twenty metres toward the net and shot the puck past Wings goalie Harry Lumley.

No one could believe what they'd witnessed. Rocket Richard scored a goal carrying a man on his back.

A month later, Richard scored goal number forty-three in the team's thirty-eighth game. The Forum crowd erupted and gave their hero the first of many standing ovations.

A week after that, Richard scored the winning goal against the Maple Leafs, tying Malone's record. Toronto fans acknowledged Richard's achievement, but the Leafs brass completely ignored it. The Leafs arena announcer said nothing. Toronto's classless act was echoed by *Globe and Mail* writer Jim Coleman: "In our book, he isn't as good a hockey player as his centre man, Elmer Lach. As for comparing him to Howie Morenz—well, it's improbable that he'll ever have Howie's gift for lifting the customers out of their seats."

Every team was out to stop Richard from setting the record. Two players were often employed to slash, taunt, trip, and provoke the Rocket into taking a penalty.

Years later, Red Storey would acknowledge the overall treatment of Richard in the league. "A lot of players weren't penalized for offences against the Rocket. They'd grab him or put a stick between his skates when the ref wasn't looking. They'd hold him by the seat of his pants when the ref was on the other side. They did all kinds of things to him, but he still scored goals."

On this night, February 25, 1945, Toronto assigned forwards Nick Metz and Bob Davidson the job of stopping the Rocket. Like tag team wrestlers, Metz and Davidson took turns shadowing the Rocket, hitting, slashing, hooking, and holding him. Unfortunately for the Leafs, they forgot that the Canadiens had other stars. Blake, Lach, and Bouchard all scored goals in what became a vicious game. There were six fights, some involving fans, and an eventual bench-clearing brawl.

The Canadiens led 4–2 with three minutes remaining in the game. Irvin wanted Richard to break the record and played him more than usual. Exhausted from the poundings and ice time, Richard had little gas left in the tank. During a faceoff, he suddenly came alive. Swinging out in front of the Leafs' net, Richard took a pass from Toe Blake and fired a waist-high shot past goalie Frank McCool.

Teammates jumped on the ice and mobbed Richard. Fourteen thousand Forum fans cheered for over ten minutes, throwing hats, fruits, pennies, and other items onto the ice. Another five thousand stood celebrating outside on the streets.

Joe Malone came out and presented the record-breaking puck to the grateful Richard. Malone was bursting with praise for Richard. "That Richard is a great hockey player. He's fast, game, and powerful. Richard would be a great hockey player in any day, age, or league."

But Richard wasn't done. He had a chance to become the first NHL player to score fifty goals in a season (which ran fifty games at the time). And he did, in typical dramatic fashion: in the final game of the season against Boston with less than two minutes left in the game.

Following a surprising loss in the first round to the weaker Maple Leafs, another tribute was held to celebrate Richard's magnificent season. Fans presented him with hundreds of gifts and money. Richard was appreciative, but the adoration wasn't enough to erase his disappointment over the team's early playoff exit.

Although the Canadiens took back the Stanley Cup in 1946, the front office decided that the team was getting older

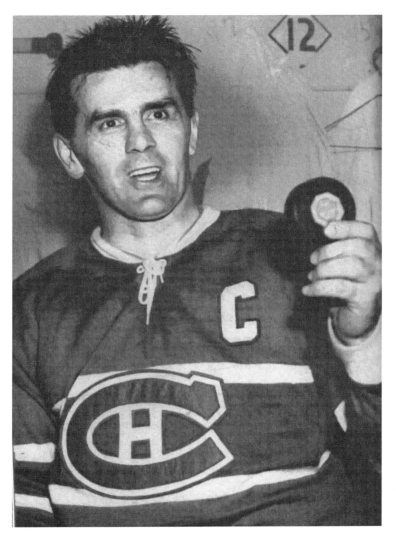

Yet another goal-scoring milestone!

and was in need of a major overhaul. The decision would see the Canadiens, led by a new crop of French-Canadian players who idolized the Rocket, reborn as one of the NHL's greatest dynasties.

Chapter 4
Rivalries

"We hate those Toronto guys so much," Canadiens forward Ray Getliffe once said, "we want to kill them."

Getliffe's words—ironic, considering he was an English-Canadian—aptly summarized the intense rivalry between the Toronto Maple Leafs and Montreal Canadiens.

The Leafs/Habs rivalry has roots that extend as far back as the Plains of Abraham, a pivotal moment in Canadian history when French-Canadians were subjected to the rule of English-Canadians.

The hockey conflict was also a reflection of the modern economic battle between the two cities over who would lead the burgeoning country. "Montrealers are beginning to fear that the geographical and economic cards are stacked against them," wrote Hugh MacLennan, "just as they fear that the mentality of Toronto is better adjusted to the modern age than their own."

French-Canadians were still a mystery to English-Canadians: they spoke a different language; they were divided between English Presbyterians and French Roman Catholics. Toronto was viewed as more conservative and uptight, whereas the French were considered to be more passionate and fiery.

Bob Haggert, the head trainer of the Maple Leafs in the 1960s, once said, "It's like stepping into another world. And the city of Montreal—it's open twenty-four hours a day. Toronto is dead—on Sunday, you can't go to a movie or a restaurant. Montreal is wide open—you can hoot and holler all day and all night long. Passion for life—that is their legacy."

Each Canadiens victory over the Leafs was a symbolic accomplishment for French Canada. "Tucked into a corner of the continent," wrote Jeffrey Simpson, "speaking a different language and feeling sorely looked down upon by English-speakers, especially in the rest of Canada, the Canadiens showed vicariously what francophone Quebeckers could accomplish."

The Canadiens were not just representative of French/English tensions, they also offered French-Canadians a

For many, the Leafs/Habs rivalry reflected the tensions between English-and French-Canadians.

respite from the internal struggles against the domineering ways of Maurice Duplessis and the Catholic church. Richard and the Habs fuelled the rebellious nature of younger

French-Canadians, giving them a sense of hope, purpose, and confidence for their future—and the future of Quebec.

The conflict between English and French Canada reached a boiling point during and following the Second World War. Many English-Canadians resented the fact that some French-Canadians refused to join the war effort.

An anonymous letter sent to Canadian military officials in 1944 is an extreme but telling revelation about the attitudes of some English-Canadians towards the French: "One cannot lose time recalling the folly of England in permitting for a moment the French retention of their language, since they were, and are, merely conquered folk permitted to remain on British terrain because of British generosity!"

Another English-Canadian who hated French-Canadians as much as the anonymous letter writer was Leafs founder and owner, Conn Smythe. Smythe left the Leafs to fight in the war, and returned with serious injuries. He quickly made headlines at home by stating that "untrained young Canadians were dying in the fields of France, Belgium, and Holland while the well-trained Zombies sat safely back at home, protected by the Liberal government." Smythe frequently called French-Canadians "frogs" and had once even begun a speech in Montreal with "Ladies, Gentlemen, and Frenchmen."

Smythe directed his xenophobic venom toward the Habs, who he felt had stacked their wartime lineup with unenlisted players. Smythe either didn't realize or accept that many Canadiens' players were supporting the cause by working in local factories. The fact that Richard (who held a wartime job as a machinist) had tried to enlist three times wasn't enough for Smythe. Smythe wondered how Richard could be healthy enough to score fifty goals in fifty games but not fight for his country.

Paradoxically, Smythe was also smitten with Richard. In 1945, Smythe attended his first NHL game since returning from the war. The Canadiens were hosting the Black Hawks. "[Frank] Selke had been telling me how terrible wartime hockey was. I had never seen the Rocket play." That night, he saw a lot of the Rocket. After the game, Smythe admonished Selke for his comments, telling him that Richard was as good a hockey player as he'd ever seen.

The next day, Smythe offered Frank Selke, now manager of the Canadiens, $25,000 for Richard's contract. The offer was swiftly rejected.

Smythe was an astute man. Money overrode politics and race. In Richard, Smythe saw, as author Douglas Hunter suggested, "a talent that can make the fans forget about the makeshift matches of the war years, a talent that can fill a rink to standing room with paying customers."

A few years later, Smythe tried again. This time he offered the Canadiens somewhere in the range of $135,000 for Richard's contract, a big amount at the time. Selke wrote

Smythe back saying "Quit cracking jokes. If disposed of Richard, the whole team would be chased out of town by our aroused fans." The offer was serious enough that the *Globe and Mail* featured an image of Richard in a Leafs' jersey on their front page.

As outrageous as the offer seemed (some thought it to be a publicity stunt on Smythe's part), Montrealers like Roch Carrier were concerned. "Will Rocket leave Montreal for Toronto? There are suspicions that Maurice and Franke Selke aren't the closest of friends. Hockey bosses, like factory workers, aren't in the habit of paying a French-Canadian what he's worth."

Incredibly, Richard would later admit that the offer was interesting to him: "It was interesting to think about what it would be like to play in Toronto. [People] believed that I represented French-speaking people of Quebec and that I couldn't conceive of playing anywhere but in Montreal." If Richard did have to leave Montreal, his first choice would be Toronto. He got on well with Smythe. "A lot of people thought we hated each other because of the rivalry between Toronto and Montreal, but the opposite was true. Even when I had my troubles in Maple Leafs Gardens, Smythe would come over and try to cool me off."

But it was merely a dream for Smythe and the Maple Leafs. The Rocket wasn't going anywhere.

Another factor in the Canadiens/Leafs rivalry was the

roles of Irvin and Selke. Both men had begun their careers with the Leafs. After a dispute between Selke and Smythe led to Selke's firing, the two men ended up with the Canadiens. Selke loved nothing more than beating the Leafs.

The Habs/Leafs rivalry had subsided to some degree during the pre-war period. But the wartime tensions between French and English Canada quickly revitalized the rivalry.

The Canadiens and Leafs met early in the 1944–45 season in Montreal. It was their first meeting since the Canadiens destroyed the Leafs 11–0 in March 1944. The game was little more than a series of brawls. Misconducts and major and minor penalties were generously given to both teams—with the majority given to the Canadiens. Montreal fans were not pleased. Former Leafs' star King Clancy was the referee, and he handed out eleven penalties to Montreal and only five to Toronto. Feeling that Clancy was biased toward the Canadiens, the Forum faithful threw papers, bottles, and even a chair onto the ice. As Clancy left the ice after the Leafs' 4–1 win, a fan punched him in the face.

The meetings between the two teams continued to be acrimonious. After pummelling the Leafs 6–0 in game one of the 1946–47 Stanley Cup finals, the Leafs entered game two looking for vengeance against the Canadiens. By the end of the first period, the Leafs were up 3–0. Part of their success stemmed from a continual pounding of Richard. Eventually, he snapped. After a collision, he took his stick and smashed

Toronto's Vic Lynn over the eye. Lynn left the game and Richard received a five-minute major.

Hostilities returned early in the second period. Richard went up against Leafs tough guy Bill Ezinicki. While a linesman stepped between the two players, Richard clubbed Ezinicki over the head with his stick. Blood dripped from Ezinicki's head. Richard was given a match penalty and a game misconduct.

Richard's temper cost his team dearly. The Canadiens played shorthanded for twenty minutes and lost the game.

The following day, NHL President Clarence Campbell suspended Richard for game three.

French-Canadians were furious over the suspension. Almost instantly, the issue of discrimination arose. A columnist for the Montreal daily, *Le Canada*, wondered why Don Metz of the Maple Leafs was only given a two-minute minor for putting Elmer Lach out for the season. "Here's indisputable proof of the influence of Smythe on the National Hockey League. Campbell is president of the league in name only, but in fact is the advocate of Conny Smythe."

Forced to listen to game three in his hotel, Richard became so angry when Ezinicki was named a game star that he tossed his radio out the window.

In the end, Richard's explosion once again cost the Canadiens. The team was unable to get back on track against a Leafs team that had become increasingly self-confident. The Leafs went on to capture the Stanley Cup with a 4–2 series win.

*Rocket's temper frequently got him into trouble. Here, teammates
and an official try to cool him down.*

Richard later admitted that he was too quick to react. "If I took a bad bodycheck, I had to retaliate, had to go after the guy right away—and I took a lot in games with the Leafs; they were the dirtiest team in the league at the time."

Though the Leafs were the Habs' rival team, Richard's most intense on-ice rivalries were with Gordie Howe and Ted Lindsay of the Detroit Red Wings.

"Everybody always wanted to compare me to Gordie Howe," Richard once said, "but I was never a natural hockey player like Gordie. He was stronger, more fluid, better with the puck. I used to say to him, 'Gordie, you're much better than I am, but you don't have the drive to win games like I do.' I always had a big heart for scoring—oh, I loved scoring goals."

"The Canadiens were our biggest rival," remembered Red Wings defencemen Marcel Pronovost. "The intensity was unbelievable. You'd walk into the Forum or the Olympia those nights, there was electricity in the air."

In those days, both teams frequently travelled on the same train during a home-and-home series. "Detroit was our biggest rival," recalled the Rocket. "I remember I used to meet their players in the aisleway of the train. We'd pass by each other and I wouldn't say hello to anybody."

"I guess any of us who played then remember those train trips when both teams would travel from Montreal to Detroit," said Ted Lindsay, one of Rocket's bitterest rivals.

"Even on the train the rivalry was there. No fights, but there were times it wasn't too far away from that."

"For me, the worst player by far whom I've ever skated against was Ted Lindsay, of the Detroit Red Wings," Richard remembered. "It wasn't so much that he was a dirty player, but as far as I am concerned, he had a dirty mouth. He swore at everybody on the ice."

It didn't take long for word to spread that to get to the Canadiens, you just needed to get Richard off his game and off the ice. "Every team used rugged methods to stop him," wrote Sidney Katz in *Maclean's*. "One—and sometimes two—players are specifically detailed to nettle him. They regularly hang on to him, put hockey sticks between his legs, body-check him, and board him harder than necessary."

Richard didn't just suffer physical abuse. Racial insults were also frequently aimed his way by coaches, players, and fans. They called him "French pea soup," "Frog," or "Dirty French Bastard."

"No hockey player has ever suffered more from illegal tactics than Maurice Richard," Canadian writer Hugh MacLennan wrote in 1955. "He is a type of player few English-speaking Canadians understand. He is that rare thing, a champion who is also an obsessed artist."

While still the Canadiens general manager, Tommy Gorman was so frustrated with the abuse Richard was taking that he wrote a letter to the NHL President, Mervyn "Red"

Dutton: "It is evident that some players are being sent on to the ice...to stop Richard by any means. Richard can defend himself against individual opponents, but not when teams become a Wreck Richard Club. Richard must be protected and we ask that the referees given him this protection."

It was the same for Richard off the ice. "He was about the most vulnerable athlete there was at the time," teammate Tom Johnson recalled. "He couldn't come out to the local bars in Detroit or Toronto with us because there would always be somebody picking a fight with him."

Richard rarely initiated rough play, but when he was on the receiving end of a dirty play, he frequently exploded. It wasn't a pretty sight. During a 1946 game against the Rangers, Richard knocked an opponent out with one punch. Instead of skating away, Richard raised his stick over the Ranger and smashed it down repeatedly beside the fallen player's head.

"A clean hit I didn't mind," Richard recalled. "A dirty hit I did mind, and ninety per cent of the time when I went after a guy, I would be the one who got the penalty."

One notorious battle took place with another New York Ranger. Defenceman Bob "Killer" Dill—the nephew of two boxers—had a reputation as one of the toughest players in hockey. Opponents feared his potent punches.

The teams were scheduled to square off a week before Christmas 1944. Sports writers, fans, and players were building up the impending battle between Dill and Richard. The newspapers featured boxing-type "Tale of the Tape" stories as they tried to predict who would come out on top.

The night arrived. The atmosphere in Madison Square Garden was tense. The fans were waiting for an epic fight. From the drop of the puck, Dill was all over Richard trying, unsuccessfully, to get him to fight.

During a second period dust-up, Dill looked at Richard and asked, "Is the frog scared?"

At last, the moment came…much to the disappointment of Rangers fans.

Richard turned and knocked Dill out with one punch.

Richard wasn't finished. On their way to the penalty box, the two players clashed a second time. Richard landed punch after punch, pummelling the dazed Dill to the ice again.

Adding a little icing on the cake, Richard came out of the box and scored the game-tying goal.

After the game, Dill met Richard and told him that it was the hardest punch he'd ever received. Richard then invited Dill out to dinner.

If Richard ever lacked fire, Irvin or a teammate would be there to light a fire under him. Irvin's son, legendary broadcaster Dick Irvin Jr., recalled that, "Dad used to say he knew when the Rocket was ready to play—his hair was standing on end."

"I always knew how to get to Rocket," said teammate Bert Olmstead. "I'd look at Dick Irvin, just before we'd go on the ice. If he nodded, I'd get on him. If he didn't, I'd leave him alone. I could handle him. I could get him so mad, but it all depended on the moment, how were doing."

Irvin's encouragement of Richard's behaviour would eventually lead to dramatic consequences.

During the 1950–51 season, Richard made headlines for his attack on referee Hugh McLean in the lobby of a hotel.

His actions followed a game where Richard battled Detroit's Leo Reise and Sid Abel. "A man can take just so much. I was skating close to the Detroit net when Sid Abel grabbed me by the chin, nearly twisted my head off, and spun me right around. I drew the referee's attention to this, but he laughed in my face."

As Richard skated away he said, "This is the damnedest thing yet." McLean immediately gave him a penalty. Skating to the penalty box, Reise taunted Richard. A big mistake. Richard threw a punch at the Red Wing and was given an additional misconduct penalty.

The following morning, Richard encountered McLean in the hotel lobby. Habs goalie Gerry McNeil, a frequent prankster, told Richard that McLean was mocking him. Richard raced across the lobby and grabbed the official by the throat. Richard tried to punch McLean before linesman Jim Primeau stepped in and began throwing punches at Richard.

Richard received a $500 fine from the NHL commissioner, Clarence Campbell. Campbell's excuse for not taking further action was that "the suspension of a great hockey star is not justified if it reflects in the gate receipts. If I suspended Richard, a great drawing card wherever he goes, it would affect the attendance of the league."

Fans weren't immune to Richard's fists either. In Detroit, he slapped a teenager who leaned over the glass to taunt him in the penalty box. "I'd slap my own son a lot harder if he dared speak to his elders that way, even at a hockey game."

Even in retirement, the Rocket continued to fight.

In 1960, the newly retired Richard went after a Maple Leaf player. "Leaf defenceman Kent Douglas hit Bobby Rousseau over the head with his stick," recalled Richard. "I was sitting just above the passageway the players go through on their way to the dressing room at the Forum. When Douglas passed underneath I tried to hit him on the head with my fist."

In 1961, he punched an obnoxious Black Hawks fan in the lobby of the Chicago stadium. The man had been heckling Richard as he sat watching the Hawks/Canadiens game. After the game, the man approached Richard and said, "I was going to challenge you to a fight after regulation time, but I chickened out."

Richard told him, "Go away. You bother me."

The man then threw a punch that grazed Richard's chin.

Richard responded with one punch. Fight over.

Worried that he might be sued by the man, Richard was approached by the man's brother.

"I'm the happiest guy in the world," said the brother. "Now that fat bully doesn't shoot his mouth off anymore and doesn't bother anybody. You did us all a service!"

For some commentators, Richard's intense play, while worshipped in Quebec, was equally feared, admired, and perplexing to English-Canadians. Author Douglas Hunter felt that to the English, Richard represented "something primal and untamed, even incomprehensible." French-Canadians, however, took hold of Richard's perceived persecution and made him the focus of their own persecution anxieties as a minority people.

One goal, often called "The Goal," perhaps best summarizes Richard's resilience and determination in the face of physical abuse.

It was the 1952 semifinals against Boston, game seven. Richard received a brutal bodycheck by Bruins defenceman Leo Labine and was down on the ice unconscious for several minutes. Blood seeped from a wound on his forehead. He was eventually helped off the ice. In the dressing room, his forehead was stitched shut.

Dizzy and wobbly, Richard insisted on returning to the Canadiens bench during the third period. He sat on the bench quiet and dazed. With four minutes remaining, Richard told

Irvin that he was ready to hit the ice. Irvin wasn't sure what to do. Richard looked completely out of it. After thinking it over, Irvin realized that this was a "win or go home" game. He sent Richard onto the ice.

The game was tied 1–1. Richard grabbed the puck in his own end and roared up the ice past the Bruins players. In the Bruins zone, Richard exploded to the front of the net, eluding the Bruins defencemen. It was now just Richard and Bruins goalie "Sugar Jim" Henry. "There were a flurry of sticks," wrote Andy O'Brien. "Henry dove, Richard pulled the puck back and blasted the netting."

"That beautiful bastard," wrote Elmer Ferguson in the *Montreal Herald*, "scored semi-conscious."

The moment was captured by the legendary photo of Henry and an almost-comatose Richard shaking hands after the game.

In the dressing room, Richard broke out in sobs. His sobs were so intense that the Canadiens' doctor had to inject him with a sedative.

He later said that the only reason he kept the puck was because his eyesight was too blurry to see his teammates.

* * *

There was a day when Toronto loved the Rocket. On October 29, 1952, Richard's pursuit of Nels Stewart's NHL record of 324 goals was on the line. Richard was at 323 heading into a game against the Leafs.

Before the game, Richard was cornered by the press. Always media shy, the perturbed Richard told the reporters, "Have you guys gone crazy? I've never had a big scoring night in your damn Gardens. Who do you think I am?"

Coach Irvin was also taken off guard by the attention. "I am stunned at the publicity that the Rocket is getting here in Toronto where, for years, fans along the rail have been yelling nasty things and grabbing his sweater; where the management has been accusing him of every crime except piracy on the high seas—you fellows have been publicizing the guff."

A crowd of over 14,000 gathered in anticipation of seeing Richard make history. Each time the puck came near Richard, the fans cheered wildly.

They weren't kept waiting for long. Eleven minutes into the game, Elmer Lach hit the speeding Rocket with a pass. The Rocket took the pass, zoomed around the stunned Leafs defence, and fired the puck behind Leafs goalie Harry Lumley. The roar of the fans was so loud, one might have thought he was in Montreal instead of Toronto. Goal number 323.

Just six minutes later, the Rocket found the puck amidst a crowd of players in front of the Leafs net and shot it past Lumley. Goal number 324.

*If ever an image summed up the fire and passion of the Rocket, it is this
iconic shot of Richard shaking hands with Boston goalie "Sugar Jim" Henry.
After suffering a head injury during the game, Richard returned to the ice
half conscious to score a dramatic overtime winning goal.*

The roar of the crowd shook Maple Leaf Gardens. Teammates jumped off the bench to congratulate the Rocket. The Gardens crowd gave Richard a standing ovation. It was an incredible and moving moment, as though a peace treaty had been signed between English and French Canada. In this moment, Leafs fans forgot about their hatred of the Canadiens, the Rocket, and, perhaps, Quebec.

Referee Red Storey gave the historic puck to a smiling Rocket, who was calm and relieved. Richard was so overwhelmed by the response he waved to the crowd in acknowledgment of their appreciation.

The Rocket was never again booed by Leafs fans.

Five years later, the Rocket scored career goal number 500. He arrived in Toronto and was greeted by Toronto Mayor Nathan Phillips, who told him, "We Canadians are very proud of you, Mr. Richard."

Chapter 5
The Richard Riot

In January 1954, Richard began writing (it was actually ghost written by a staff reporter) "Le Tour du Chapeau" ("Hat trick"), a sports column for the French weekly *Samedi-Dimanche*. In the column, Richard didn't hold back in his criticisms. First he called Quebec City fans "hoodlums" for their treatment of brother Henri in a junior game. The attack caused a stir to the point where the Quebec provincial legislature discussed and denounced Richard's accusations.

But it would be the next column that would be the most memorable, and that undoubtedly had a serious effect on the relationship between Richard and NHL President Clarence Campbell.

Richard commented on a vicious stick-swinging fight between teammate Boom Boom Geoffrion and Ron Murphy of the New York Rangers. Although Campbell admitted that Murphy (who suffered a broken jaw) was the instigator, he gave Geoffrion an eight-game suspension, and Murphy only five games.

Richard charged that Geoffrion's punishment was excessive and that Campbell's actions were further evidence of his "evident partiality" to Canadiens' opponents:

> *What a farce! It would be funny if it wasn't so tough on Geoffrion, one of the stars of the league and a gentleman as well. I'll go no further. According to friends who watch President Campbell during games at the Forum, he shows evident partiality in his reactions to the play. He smiles and openly shows pleasure when an opposing club scores against us, and it is known that on several occasions he has given his decision against Canadien players.*
>
> *What did Campbell do when Jean Béliveau was deliberately injured twice by players*

The Richard Riot

> *from Chicago and New York? No penalty, no*
> *fine, no suspension. Did he suspend Gordie*
> *Howe of Detroit when he almost knocked*
> *out Dollard St-Laurent's eye two years ago?*
> *No!*

> *It is strange that only Dick Irvin and I*
> *have the courage to risk our livelihood by*
> *defending our rights against such a dictator.*

Finally, Richard cut to what he felt was the real reason behind Campbell's bias: "Let Campbell get busy with other little goings-on known about players of the National Hockey League and not try to create publicity at the expense of a good fellow like Boom Boom Geoffrion just because he is a French-Canadian."

Clarence Campbell was not pleased.

But Richard's temperament didn't end on the printed page. On the ice, Richard was becoming increasingly volatile.

During a game against the Leafs on December 29, 1954, "Hockey's smouldering volcano," wrote Milt Dunnell in the *Toronto Star*, "erupted again, showering fire, ash and expletives all over the Gardens."

Late in the game, Richard exploded on the Leafs' Bob Bailey. "He was mad," recalled the game's official, Red Storey, "because Bailey tried to gouge his eyes out. Rocket just went berserk."

Maurice Richard

Richard chased the Leafs forward around the ice and slammed his stick into his face. The two men fell to the ice. Bailey began pummelling Richard. The linesman pulled them apart. Richard, eyes still ablaze, attempted to free himself and attack Bailey with his stick again. Finally, he broke free of the officials and smacked one of them across the face with his glove.

Richard was given a five-minute major and two ten-minute misconducts. Clarence Campbell then slapped Richard with a $250 fine.

Little was made of the incident. The Habs were having a great season. Richard was leading the league in scoring, heading toward his first scoring championship. The Habs were, by far, the top team in the league.

Everything was running smoothly until March 13, 1955. It was the second game of a home-and-home series with the Boston Bruins. Following a hard-hitting first game that left Richard with a sore back and insomnia, the teams headed back to Boston to close out the series.

Late in the game, Richard and former teammate Hal Laycoe engaged in a vicious stick swinging battle. "Rocket came down the ice," former Bruin Fleming Mackell told Dick Irvin Jr., "and high-sticked Laycoe at the blue line. Laycoe hit him back. He dropped his stick on Richard's head. Blood started seeping from Richard's head. When Richard saw the blood he went nuts. They start swinging sticks at each other's heads. It was frightening."

Linesman Cliff Thompson, a former Bruin, jumped in and tried to hold Richard. Canadiens defenceman Doug Harvey then grabbed Thompson, freeing Richard. Richard immediately grabbed another stick and attacked Laycoe again. Laycoe didn't have his stick and desperately tried to protect himself.

But Thompson got hold of Richard a second time. Richard thought the official was trying to restrain him so that Laycoe could keep punching him. Richard turned around and swung at Thompson. "The official was holding me from behind," Richard said later, "and I warned him two or three times. The fourth time, I turned around and poked him." Thompson ended up with a black eye. Richard was tossed from the game.

"You couldn't hear a sound," recalled Mackell, "Everything was so quiet. Over half the crowd got up and left the building. Fans were scared. That's the only time I ever saw fans act like that."

"It was unfortunate, really, what happened," Laycoe said later. "There were no ill feelings between Rocket and me. Hell, we used to play tennis together."

Two Boston officers appeared outside the Canadiens' dressing room to arrest Richard on a charge of assault and battery with a dangerous weapon. Irvin blocked the door and a heated argument took place. The police officers left only after they were promised that the league would look into the issue.

Three days later, a meeting took place in Clarence Campbell's office. Richard, the game officials, Boston General Manager Lynn Patrick, and Canadiens Assistant General Manager Ken Reardon were all in attendance.

Everyone knew Richard would be suspended. It was expected to be along the lines of Ted Lindsay's recent four-game suspension for punching a fan.

"I knew before we went in that he was gone," Reardon recalled. "There had been an owners meeting the day before. I believe that it was decided there that Rocket was gone. The owners said he was getting too big for hockey and he was gone."

Campbell gave his verdict: "Whether this type of conduct is the product of temperamental instability or willful defiance of authority of the game does not matter. Richard will be suspended from all games, both league and playoffs, for the balance of the season."

French-Canadians were outraged; the city was in shock. A Montreal *Gazette* employee cried. A bus was nearly hit by a train because of a distracted driver. A man called the NHL office with a message for Campbell: "Tell Campbell I'm an undertaker and he'll be needing me in a few days." A Progressive-Conservative Member of Parliament even tried to introduce the Richard suspension into the House of Commons, but the topic was refused. People called Richard at home, some telling him that they'd get Campbell. He told the fans to calm down, but knew it was to no avail.

The Richard Riot

Habs fans express their feelings toward NHL President Clarence Campbell.

"After the announcement," recalled Dick Irvin Jr., "'Kill Campbell' became the slogan of the day throughout Montreal. The NHL offices received bomb threats. Signs were put up with pictures of Campbell as a pig, etc..." The main gathering point was the Forum, where crowds, hatred, and trouble grew to huge proportions all during the day and through to game time.

The suspension triggered individual memories of humiliation and indignity in French-Canadians. They talked about working for bosses like Clarence Campbell, who cheated

77

them out of wages. They remembered places they were not welcome because of their ethnicity. For these people, humiliating the Rocket was a slap in their face.

On March 17, 1955, against his better judgment—and warnings from Montreal Mayor Jean Drapeau—Campbell decided to attend the Canadiens home game against the Detroit Red Wings. Accompanied by his secretary, Phyllis, Campbell took his usual seat near the goal judge.

"It was my first night covering an NHL game," recalled Montreal *Gazette* columnist Red Fisher. "I was assigned to sit in the stands and write a mood piece, how the fans were feeling, etc...I got a seat ten rows back of the Red Wings' bench. You could feel the tension prior to the game. Ten seconds into the game I got hit by an egg. This was my welcome to the NHL."

People threw fruits, vegetables, eggs, overshoes, hot dogs, ice cubes, pickles, potatoes, and tomatoes in Campbell's direction. One man approached Campbell and squashed tomatoes on him.

Richard's suspension didn't only affect the fans. It was obvious that even the players weren't the same. The Wings came out of the gate flying and were up 4–0 in the first period. The crowd became even more agitated.

At the end of the first period, a man walked over to Campbell and extended his hand as if to shake hands. As Campbell put his hand out, the man slapped him across the face.

All hell broke lose and a tear-gas bomb was thrown. Panic erupted. People began hacking and coughing and scrambling for the exits.

The game was forfeited to the Red Wings.

Outside the Forum, thousands of protestors awaited. Men, women, and children, young and old, from different classes, all angry with Campbell and the treatment of Richard. People sat on cars, phone booths, newsstands, trees. More anti-Campbell signs could be seen, bearing slogans like: "Campbell, Drop Dead"; "Richard is being persecuted"; "Outrageous decision"; "Injustice against French Canada"; "Stupid Puppet Campbell."

The combination of panic, anger, and tear gas had set off a riot. Windows were broken. A gun was fired. Cars were overturned. Anything that could be thrown was hurled in the direction of the Forum. The sound of breaking glass filled the air. The barrage was so concentrated that police supervising the evacuation inside had to turn several thousand spectators around and escort them out via the side exits. Cars, taxis, and buses on St. Catherine and Atwater became moving targets. Wails of sirens clashed with street music. Several police cars were heavily damaged, and more than once a policeman who had arrested wrongdoers had to surrender his prisoners when surrounded by crowds of rioters.

"By 3 a.m.," Sidney Katz wrote in *Maclean's*, "the last rock had been hurled, the last window had been smashed, the

Tear gas fills the Forum.

last blood-curdling shriek of 'Kill Campbell' had been uttered. The fury of the mob had been spent."

During the four-hour riot, 10,000 people took to the

streets, looting and vandalizing. Thirty-seven people were arrested. A dozen policemen and twenty-five rioters were injured. Damage was estimated to be over $100,000.

Richard only learned of the riot later, on the radio.

The next day, Richard goes on radio and television to appeal to his fans for calm: "I want to do what is good for the people of Montreal and my team. So that no further harm will be done, I would like to ask everyone to get behind the team and help the boys win..."

The people listened. There was no more talk of riots or revenge.

But as was typical in the rivalry, English and French newspapers took opposite sides.

The Canadian Press wire agency called the riot, "The worst seen in Montreal since the anti-conscription riots which marked the last war."

The riot was covered across North America and around the world. Papers in London, Berlin, and Dublin all covered the story. In Dublin, the paper joked that the French-Canadians had thrown a better St. Patrick's Day party than was ever seen in Ireland.

In Montreal, everyone found someone to blame for the riot.

"Let me tell you who I blame for all this," said Detroit General Manager Jack Adams to reporters. "I blame you fellows for what happened. You've turned Richard into an idol, a man who's suspension can turn hockey fans into shrieking idiots. Now hear this: Richard is no hero! He let his team down. He let his public down. He let the league down. And he let hockey down."

A city councilman demanded the resignation of the police chief. Another wanted a warrant for the arrest of Campbell, saying that he had provoked the riot.

While Mayor Jean Drapeau didn't go that far, he did release a statement stating that Campbell should not have attended the game or at the very least, not announced publicly that he'd be there.

Campbell shot back: "Does the Mayor suggest I should have yielded to the intimidation of a few hoodlums? What a strange and sorry commentary from the chief magistrate of our city who was sworn to uphold the law, and who as senior officer of the civic administration is responsible for the protection of the property of the citizens through our police force."

Four days later in *Le Devoir*, Andre Laurendeau wrote:

> *The crowds that vented their anger last*
> *Thursday night were not motivated solely by*
> *passions of sport or an injustice committed*
> *against an idol. It was a frustrated people*
> *who protested against their fate. Their fate,*
> *in this instance, was called Mr. Campbell*

*and he was the incarnation of all the
adversaries, real or imagined, of this small
people.*

*We are suddenly tired of always having
masters, of having for a long time been
beaten down. Mr. Campbell is going to see.
One does not have every day weak sorts
between the hands, one cannot every day
wring someone's neck without bad luck.*

*Without doubt, the death today is
symbolic...But this brief flare-up betrays
what lies behind the apparent indifference
and long passivity of the French-Canadians.*

Andy O'Brien, author of *Rocket Richard*, felt that the city had changed after the riots: "I found definite hostility rising between French and English factions. The city was tersely split. I have never seen so many normally upper-intelligent people talking so wild-eyedly and using arguments that would normally not be contemplated, much less voiced, by morons. On the English as well as the French side everybody was mad, clean through, deep-down boiling mad."

There were costs on the ice as well.

Richard was still leading the league in scoring. With two games left, teammate Boom Boom Geoffrion was a close second. Many fans didn't want Geoffrion to overtake Richard's quest for a first scoring championship (and its $1000 bonus).

When Geoffrion scored two points to surpass the Rocket by one point for the championship, he became a target for abuse in Montreal. Some fans never forgave him.

"It wasn't my fault Richard got suspended," Geoffrion wrote years later. "What do you want me to do? We were going at the time for first place between us and Detroit. I remember Doug Harvey and Big Jean [Béliveau] saying to me, 'Hey Boom, that doesn't mean that when you get the chance to score you miss the net just because it's Rocket.'"

Afterward, Geoffrion was forced to hire police protection after his wife and kids received threats.

Richard later wrote a very revealing take on the Geoffrion controversy: "I certainly can't blame the Boomer. He was trying to win games for the team. He was also playing to win the scoring championship, but there were a few assists that he received over the season that were cheap. When I think of them and the fact that it was my last chance at the title, I can't help but feel resentful."

Surprisingly, the Rocket-less Habs took the Red Wings to seven games in the Stanley Cup finals. It was a testament to the new crop of youngsters like Geoffrion, Béliveau, Dickie Moore, and Doug Harvey. The Richard Riot not only changed

Richard and Quebec, it also changed the Montreal Canadiens —for the better.

Over the years, many opinions have been voiced about both the fairness of the suspension and the impact of the Richard Riot on Quebec society.

"Based on the ill-handling of the situation by Thompson and the provocation delivered by Laycoe," wrote Stan Fischler in *The Flying Frenchmen*, "the Rocket's penalty was unfair in the extreme and a classic example of Campbell's negative treatment of Richard."

The normally mild-mannered Jean Béliveau stated bluntly that he believed that "the other five teams had ganged up on the Canadiens. All these gentlemen demanded that something be done to curb Maurice Richard, whose greatest fault was defeating their teams and filling their arenas to capacity."

In 1983, Frank Selke admitted that he had "not shaken the feeling that certain people felt it was time to punish Richard for the way he acted on the ice. Although I hoped for the best, I expected the worst when Campbell announced his decision."

And how did the Rocket feel about the suspension? "First of all, I didn't deserve that much, that kind of a suspension. The linesman was the problem. After that, he was out of the league and never worked there again. He was the one that was to blame."

Until his dying day, Campbell carried no regrets about his actions. Many others swear that his action was a calculated slap against the Canadiens, Richard, and French-Canadians in general.

In his book, *Maurice Richard*, Charles Foran suggests that Campbell failed to understand Richard's grievances, character, and community. It didn't help matters that Campbell worked out of the Sun Life building, a symbol of English financial dominance, and lived in the English-dominated neighbourhood of Westmount. He was perceived as a "colonial administrator."

Over fifty years later, many French-Canadians see the Richard Riot as a turning point in the development of Quebec society.

"If, at the time," Rejean Tremblay of *La Presse* wrote, "many Anglophones were unwilling to acknowledge that the Campbell-Richard confrontation had political consequences, I don't think that is the case today. Too many people say Quebec's Quiet Revolution did not begin in 1960 with the arrival of Jean Lesage and the Liberals, but with the Richard Riots. That told us that the backhanded attitude of the English establishment would no longer be tolerated."

During a 1999 Radio-Canada broadcast, Jean-Claude Lord (quoted in Benoît Melançon's *The Rocket: A Cultural History of Maurice Richard*) connects the riot to the Duplessis years of iron-fisted rule: "We were living in a closed space, where the clergy, the Church ran everything. So you had the gut feeling of frustration that we wanted to get rid of, we wanted to shout it out, that we could do other things, too."

Maurice Richard embodied those frustrated desires.

But just how ethnic was the riot? There were many English Montrealers participating in the riot along with various criminals, looters, and angry youth who were just there to take advantage of the hostile settings.

Many English- and French-Canadians adored the Rocket. In a March 21, 1955 article, Andre Laurendeau admitted that "there can be little doubt that all hockey fans, whatever their nationality, admire Richard's style of play... There would certainly have been English speakers among those outraged by Mr. Campbell's decision."

Richard's actions against Laycoe and Thompson could not be defended. His inability to control his emotions—regardless of the abuse he took every game—cost both himself and his team. When Campbell mentioned "temperamental instability" some believed he was insulting French-Canadians, but isn't it possible that he was referring to Richard's emotional state?

"To many observers elsewhere in Canada and in professional hockey," wrote Charles Foran, "Clarence Campbell was actually doing his best to negotiate the erratic and exasperating behaviour of a star athlete with an alarming temper and a lack of self-discipline."

Paradoxically, the person who mattered least in the fallout from the Richard Riot was the man who inspired it. The moment the riot occurred, Richard's beliefs were irrelevant. He was at the mercy of those with historical, cultural, and political agendas.

"The Riot is one of the pillars of the Maurice Richard myth," wrote Benoît Melançon. "Richard's role in the events of that day was peripheral, but those same events had a lasting impact on people's recollections, and on the stories they would go on to tell. Had there been no Riot, it is doubtful there would ever have been a Maurice Richard myth."

Richard seemed keenly aware of the realities of the riot: "I realize I was important to a lot of people as a symbol, but I could not look at the politics of it. I was a hockey player; I have always been a hockey player. When you talk about politics, you talk about people manipulating things that happened, a long time after they happened."

Nevertheless, the Richard Riot changed the lives of Richard and French-Canadians. In a way, the riot signalled the death of Maurice Richard the person, and the birth of Rocket Richard the myth. He had become an essential part of the fabric of change in Quebec—whether he liked it or not.

While Richard's impact off the ice was seen as merely symbolic, on the ice, it was real. Heading out of the fires of

the riot and into the autumn of change, Richard was determined to lead a young group of French-Canadian superstars
to victory.

Chapter 6
Winds of Change

When Frank Selke took over the Canadiens' general manager position in 1946, the team had few French-Canadian players. In fact, they had few players in their system. Selke set about constructing a farm system with a team in every province.

With the approval of Canadiens' owner Senator Donat Raymond, Selke set about building a network of Montreal-sponsored teams in Nova Scotia, Ontario, Manitoba, Saskatchewan, Alberta, and Quebec. Quebec was, naturally, a particularly important area to Selke.

"We had to do two things," said Selke. "Build an organization which on one hand could recruit the very best talent available across Canada, and at the same time develop the pool of players in our backyard, Quebec."

Selke's investment would reap huge dividends by the 1950s, providing Richard with a stellar supporting cast of Quebec-born talent that included future hall-of-famers Jean Béliveau, Bernie Geoffrion, Dickie Moore, Doug Harvey, Jacques Plante, and the Rocket's younger brother, Henri.

The Rocket had grown up idolizing—and later playing with and for—Toe Blake. In turn, Rocket's rise to stardom inspired this new generation of Quebec hockey players. Now, they were playing with their idol. "The Rocket was the heart and soul of the Canadiens," wrote Jean Béliveau, "an inspiration to us all and especially to younger French-Canadians who were rising through the ranks. He was man and myth, larger than life in some ways, yet most extraordinarily human in others."

Camille Desroches said, "They were proud of what they meant to the community and they got involved. When it came time to play hockey, they had more at stake than players on a lot of others teams."

Although Doug Harvey joined the Canadiens in 1948, he didn't hit his peak until 1954.

Bernie Geoffrion joined the Canadiens in 1951. He was known for his wicked slapshot and gregarious sense of humour. During his junior days, Geoffrion began lifting his stick to slap the puck (rather than the common wrist shot).

The overwhelming power of his slapshot led people to nickname Geoffrion "Boom Boom."

Unfortunately, Geoffrion (who was still considered a rookie because he played only eighteen games the previous year) was having an outstanding season. Irvin couldn't stop praising Boom Boom: "The kid is better than Rocket was in his first season."

"When the Canadiens were on the radio," recalled Geoffion in his autobiography, *Boom Boom: The Life and Times of Bernard Geoffrion*, "I would listen for every mention of the Rocket. For me, nobody could be bigger than Maurice Richard, and when he scored the roar of the crowd was music to my ears." And now, Geoffrion was playing alongside his idol.

The young Geoffrion once had the opportunity to meet his hero. Geoffrion told him: "Mr. Richard, you are my idol. I listen to you on the radio all the time. I am going to work hard and I want to be just like you."

Richard replied: "I hope you make it one day, kid."

Richard's words proved prophetic. Geoffrion (like Richard) would one day be playing alongside his idol.

In December 1951, Selke brought up another prospect: Montrealer Dickie Moore. Moore was a feisty player with scoring skills and grit. Moore's impact was immediate. He scored twenty-nine points in just twenty-seven games and was a candidate for rookie of the year.

The centrepiece of the new Quebec stars was Jean Béliveau. The Canadiens had chased their prized prospect for years without success. Béliveau was enjoying stardom and success with the Quebec Aces of the Quebec Senior Hockey League. Eventually, after the Canadiens purchased the entire league, they turned it pro, leaving Béliveau—whom the Habs owned the rights to—no other choice but to play for them.

Like Rocket and Geoffrion, Béliveau was an instant target. In his first season, he was hit hard during a game against Chicago. Béliveau missed twenty-six games.

In goal was the equally eccentric, but brilliant, Jacques Plante. Plante was a cocky loner. He knitted toques and was a hypochondriac to the point where he often stayed in a different hotel from the rest of the Canadiens because of his asthma.

On the ice, Plante revolutionized the game. He was the first goaltender to regularly wear a mask. In order to better enable his defencemen to get the puck of the zone, he skated behind his net to stop the puck and either control it for a defenceman or pass it to a teammate. He was the first to do this.

"He's the kind of athlete who is unbeatable when he *wants* to play the game. I like Jacques better as a player than as a personality. He popped off to the press and never seem to want to take blame for anything. Some of the players developed a dislike for him."

Richard and his teammates endured their eccentric netminder because, as Toe Blake said, "For five seasons he was the greatest goalie the league had ever seen."

Finally, there was Richard's brother, Henri. Fifteen years younger than the Rocket, Henri barely knew his superstar brother. But he certainly didn't need his help to become a professional hockey player.

Henri, soon nicknamed the "Pocket Rocket," arrived in the Habs camp when he was only nineteen years old. The thinking was that the Habs brass would take a look at the young Richard and then send him to one of their farm teams.

Henri had different ideas. Playing on a line with Rocket and Dickie Moore during training camp, Henri dominated the ice with his speed and skills. No one could get the puck away from him.

Blake had seen enough. Pocket Rocket wasn't going anywhere. The teenager made the Canadiens.

Despite the incredible depth of the talent, there was no doubt who led the team.

"As players," wrote Béliveau, "we saw Maurice in simpler, more immediate terms. He embodied a force, an energy, something that rubbed off on many of his teammates and carried us to five straight championships by the end of the decade. Maurice Richard hated to lose, with every fibre of his being, and his fever was infectious."

"We were just too good to hold down for too long," said

Doug Harvey. "We had all of these super young players and we were very hungry. On top of that, the Rocket was like a bomb ready to go off. He was robbed out of the scoring title the year before and he was damned if he was going to lose anything again."

The timing of his accomplishments, from the war years to 1960, coincided with that period in Quebec when a tidal wave of social change was sweeping aside more than three hundred years of history. He became a cultural icon.

"Maurice was more than a hockey player. He was a hero who defined a people emerging from an agrarian society in the post-war era and moving to the cities to seek their fortunes," Jean Béliveau said. "For those people, he became a cultural icon."

Interestingly, it was a combination of English and French stars who would go on to help the Canadiens become one of the greatest teams in hockey history. In 1971, Richard wrote, "There was never any trouble between the French-speaking players and the English-speaking players. In all the eighteen years I spent with the team there was never an argument between a Frenchman and an Englishman."

In fact, the great Canadiens team of the 1970s was also led by a combination of French (Guy Lafleur, Serge Savard, Yvan Cournoyer) and English (Ken Dryden, Larry Robinson, Steve Shutt) stars.

However, now, in the messy aftermath of the Richard

Richard was adored by children throughout Quebec and the rest of Canada.

Riot, Frank Selke decided he'd had enough of Dick Irvin's aggressive coaching tactics. While Irvin has to be credited with guiding the Rocket to fame and success, it was also felt that he had encouraged his star's violent acts. In fact, Leafs owner Conn Smythe had proof. During a game between the Leafs and Habs, a minor scuffle took place. At one point, Richard skated to the bench and Irvin spoke to him. Richard skated back to the ice and attacked a Leafs player with his stick.

"I could not help but think," Selke wrote years later, "that Dick's penchant for goading Richard had altogether too much to do with getting the great star in the mood that touched off all the trouble. And when Dick launched into another tirade at President Campbell, after we lost our final game of the season, I had made up my mind."

After fifteen years as the greatest coach in Canadiens history, Dick Irvin was sent packing.

Selke offered Irvin another job in the organization, but the coach refused. Instead, he took over the coaching duties for the Chicago Black Hawks in the 1955–56 season. Sadly, no one knew that Irvin was dying of cancer. He succumbed to the disease in 1957.

Richard was not pleased with the decision to let Irvin go. "He was like a second father to me." He also called the accusations that Irvin was encouraging his explosive temper, "a lot of bunk. I think that what happened would have happened if anybody else was behind the bench."

Throughout the summer of 1955, there was speculation about whom Selke would hire to replace Irvin.

"The board of directors," said Selke, "and the French-Canadian players wanted a French coach. I could sympathize with these people; French Canada was supplying so many wonderful hockey players and yet no one was giving jobs to French-Canadian coaches who were as good as anybody around."

If Montreal Canadiens didn't hire French-Canadian coaches, who would?

What did Selke do? After consulting with Richard, Selke hired his star's former teammate and hero, Toe Blake. Blake had coaching experience, knew the players and, most importantly, was bilingual.

Richard couldn't have been happier. "Most of the team had played with Toe. They knew the kind of competitor he was, a fellow who hated to lose, who knew his hockey, and was liked by everyone who ever met him."

There was good harmony on the club. After the disappointments of the last two seasons—along with the scar of the Richard Riot—the Canadiens were a determined bunch entering the 1955–56 season.

And Richard knew that something had to change.

"I made up my mind that I was going to work at controlling my temper and would stay out of trouble at all costs. I realized that I would be doing myself and the team a lot of good by concentrating on hockey and hockey alone."

Before the season, Selke told the Rocket, "You no longer

have anything to prove either to the other players, the fans, or to me. Through the lean years you carried the team on your back. It's time for the younger players to help out, especially when it gets to roughhouse stuff."

Blake's first job was to calm the Rocket down. "I often had to cool him out, right on the bench. He glared at me, but he took it. Maybe because I was an old linemate and he knew we had been through a lot together, and most likely because he didn't want to make my first season as an NHL coach tougher."

But it wasn't easy.

After a particularly nasty encounter with Rangers' goon Lou Fontinato that left Richard with a bloody left eye, he sat in the dressing room seething with rage. Former teammate Ken Reardon, now the Canadiens' Vice-President, sensed trouble. He raced to the dressing room, approached Richard, and told him: "Everybody here knows we can't risk—for the team's sake—another serious jam that might lose you for the Canadiens."

In the season following the riot, Richard's penalty minutes dropped and he scored thirty-eight goals. He replaced Butch Bouchard as captain. During his five-year captaincy, the Canadiens won an incredible five straight Stanley Cups, a record that remains unbroken.

Not surprisingly, Richard let his play do his talking. "The Rocket led by example, by putting the puck in the net," said

Dickie Moore. "All the players in the room were in awe of him; they were in awe of how forceful he was in pleasing the people."

Blake was a tough coach, but his players respected him. They wanted to play well for him. Aiding the cause was a formidable roster that Selke put together.

"Sometimes it's tough to coach players you once had as teammates. But these fellas went out of their way to make it easy for me. Even from the beginning we were like one big family." With the exception of the Rocket and Jacques Plante, the players frequently went out together after games.

The 1950s was a new beginning of sorts for the Canadiens. The Rocket was beginning to prepare the new stars for their years ahead. With the talent on hand, the Canadiens went on to unprecedented success.

Richard had been named captain of his formidable team in the 1956–57 season. Despite his quiet demeanor, he was most certainly a leader to the new, younger players.

In Benôit Melançon's book *The Rocket: A Cultural History of Maurice Richard*, Béliveau wrote about Richard, "Beside me in the dressing room he said very little, even after I had been a member of the team for some time. But he treated me well, like any other member of the team, and that was all a younger player could ask for. It was on the ice that Maurice did his talking, where his leadership stood out. His offensive exploits were an inspiration to all of us."

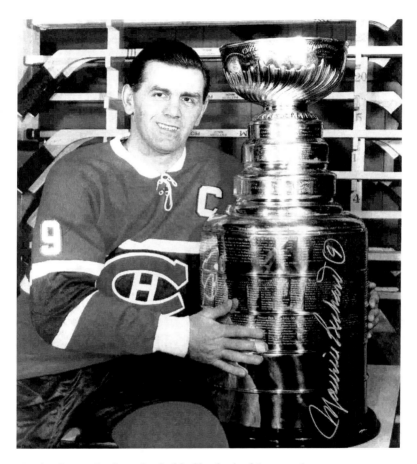

A calm, happy Rocket takes hold of hockey's ultimate prize.

The team that had been assembled in the early 1950s was taking shape nicely. In 1956, the Canadiens hoisted the Cup after defeating the Detroit Red Wings. Plante had played a spectacular final game. Richard, Geoffrion, and Béliveau had all scored. There was no doubt about the talent on this team.

But the Canadiens didn't end it there. The following season, they beat out the Boston Bruins, raising their ninth Stanley Cup. And there was more to follow. The Canadiens went on to win the Cup another three times—five times in a row. Something that had never been done.

By 1960, the Canadiens had made it to the playoffs ten years in a row. Some people, although acknowledging the success of a team of stars, were finding their victories tiresome. *Sports Illustrated* was one of them: "Next season, it would be refreshing if by some remarkable stroke of luck Montreal crumbled and the Stanley Cup ended up on a shelf in some other city."

Even though the team was counting up the Cups, it was evident that Richard was coming to the end of his game. He had been injured in most of those seasons. And in the 1959 playoffs, he didn't even score. In the 1960 playoffs, he had scored just once.

There was most certainly change on the horizon. But it wasn't a change that Richard was very happy to make.

Chapter 7
Legacy

"I am afraid of my future," Richard told June Callwood in a 1959 article in *Maclean's* magazine. "I am afraid to grow older. I never used to think of it. Now it's on my mind every day. I will be so lonely when hockey is over for me."

He must have known that day was fast approaching. His career was resembling its beginnings. He was riddled with injuries. In 1956, he injured his elbow and had minor surgery. In 1957, he missed forty-two games because of an Achilles tendon injury. He missed most of the 1958–59 season with a broken leg. In 1959–60, a facial fracture knocked him out for nineteen games.

Richard's ongoing struggle with his weight was not helping matters. During the last five years of his career, he weighed over 200 pounds (as compared to 160 when he started with the Canadiens). "With my weight," recalled Richard, "I just wasn't the same Rocket. I tried dieting a couple of times and lost about ten pounds each time, but it made me feel weak."

In the last few seasons, Richard was, incredibly, being booed by some fans (the schizophrenic reaction of Habs fans continues to this day). It was shocking to Richard, but he also saw it as a sign that maybe it was time to hang up his skates.

During the off-season in 1960, Selke told Richard, "If you needed the money badly or we were desperate for manpower, we probably would be urging you to play another season. Since neither of these conditions exist, I must tell you we are concerned about the possibility of you getting hurt badly."

Richard appeared to ignore Selke's advice when he showed up for training camp in September 1960. "When I arrived at the 1960 training camp I surprised myself," recalled Richard. "I played very well and was scoring goals, but also I was feeling it. I was obviously forcing myself and I seemed to be trying too hard. Back on the bench I'd get dizzy spells. And I started to fear getting hurt. Right in the middle of training camp I made up my mind that I had had it. The dizziness, the pushing, and the fact that it was so hard to lose weight convinced me that I'd be better off retiring."

For his farewell performance, Richard fired four goals

past Jacques Plante during a scrimmage. Then he left the ice and retired.

After giving up the goals, Plante said, "If the Rocket was too old and didn't have 'it' anymore, what did that make me, huh?"

Years later, Richard admitted that he wasn't ready to retire. "I would have loved to keep going, and probably should have tried harder."

And Richard and Quebec seemed to be entwined. Just as Richard had announced his resignation from hockey in 1960, the province was on the brink of change. The "Quiet Revolution," begun with the Liberal slogan *"C'est le temps que ça change"* ("It's time for a change"), seemed to echo Richard's decision to step away from the game. Richard's absence seemed to signal a rebirth for Quebec.

Selke immediately offered Richard a job within the organization as the team's ambassador. That night Richard went home, put on a suit, and went to the Queen Elizabeth Hotel to face the media for the announcement. He answered questions for five minutes. When he was done, the media gave him a standing ovation. Whether it was modesty or the realization that his playing career had come to a close, the quiet Richard slipped out of the room.

His stint as the team's vice-president didn't last long when he quickly realized that he was little more than a figure-head. "Apparently, the new administration didn't want me to do anything. I was just a showpiece sitting around the Forum like a potted plant. The only thing I was to do was go to the occasional banquet and make a few speeches, at half the salary I made before." After four years of frustration, Richard resigned.

The split with the Canadiens lasted until 1980, when he returned to the organization to serve as ambassador.

But Richard tried, unsuccessfully, to venture outside of the hockey world. He opened a tavern (his anger toward the Canadiens and the Molson family—who owned the team—was so strong that he refused to sell Molson beer), only to close it three years later. He toured the country as part of the NHL's old-timers squad and seemed almost surprised to discover that he was a hockey icon from coast to coast to coast. He then took a sales job for a home heating company. What an incredible experience it must have been for homeowners when the great Rocket came to their door.

In 1967, he started a fishing line business. In 1972, he became the first coach of the new rival league World Hockey Association's Quebec Nordiques. He lasted two games before he resigned for "health reasons." Later he would admit that it was simply an excuse because he was uneasy about being away from his family and home. But he continued to be a hockey presence, refereeing games. He even appeared in commercials for a hair dye company. One remains famous to this day: "Hey, Richard, two minutes for looking so good!"

Legacy

But all these ventures would never make him truly happy. They could never ignite the fire in his fierce eyes, and he could never give those endeavours the determination and soul that he had lent to hockey, to the game that he once acknowledged as being "the most important thing in my life."

Maurice "Rocket" Richard, now retired, did not fade into oblivion. In 1961, just one year after his retirement, the Hockey Hall of Fame waived its traditional three-year waiting period to induct the hockey legend.

The Rocket's legendary status carried on, into the '70s, throughout the '80s, and well into the '90s. He was still idolized; today, perhaps even more so. Books have been written about him, movies made. New generations of fans have been born. They hear tales of his five-goal night; of scoring while carrying Earl Siebert on his back; of his most devoted fans causing a riot in the streets of Montreal.

Today's fans may be left to watch replays on television or read biographies of the man who had ignited a province, but his importance to the people of Quebec is not entirely lost.

"The Rocket is not just a hockey player, he's a true piece of Canadiana," wrote Jeffrey Morris, of *Beckett Hockey Card Monthly* in 1998.

Richard transformed hockey in Quebec with his godlike status. Richard once said, "I think I'm human, just like everybody else." But he wasn't. He was larger than life to most.

Quebec filmmaker Bernard Gosselin remembers

growing up and meeting the Rocket. One of his neighbours, a tailor, had one of the first plate-glass windows in his store. One day, Gosselin and his friends looked inside and spotted Richard trying on clothes. They all ran to the window and peered in at their idol, trying on clothes just like anyone else. "We'd have been less excited to see the pope," he recalled.

Then Richard stopped what he was doing and walked outside. "What do you want?" he asked.

"We want to see Maurice Richard," the boys said.

Richard looked at them and said, "Maurice Richard? Who's that?" But he stayed with the boys for an hour, talking and having fun with them.

Sitting and enjoying time with the hero of Quebec. "It was fantastic and unexpected," Gosselin said.

Richard may not have been the most talented man on the ice during his years in the NHL. But he most certainly made himself a force to be reckoned with. Through his sheer will and determination, he made himself the best player on the ice. The clutch player. The one you knew you could count on.

What made Richard stand out above other, more talented players was his desire and passion. He made a point of doing what he loved well. He was an artist on the ice and brought his sense of drama and passion to the fans in the stands. His five-goal game against the Maple Leafs in 1944, where he was named all three stars, became a thing of legend.

Even Richard's enemy, Clarence Campbell, recognized

his presence: "He entertained me more than any other player. You couldn't remain indifferent when Richard was on the ice."

To this day, Richard's influence on hockey is more than evident.

Fifty goals in fifty games became the benchmark for NHL players. But it was a lofty goal: it took the next player thirty-six years to reach it, when Mike Bossy reached the milestone in the 1980–81 season. Richard sent the ecstatic player a telegram of congratulations that night.

Reaching 500 goals in a career is another milestone players seek to reach. Gordie Howe did it five years after Richard. It would take another eight years for someone else to reach that goal.

Richard's contribution to hockey couldn't go unnoticed. On January 24, 1999, the Maurice "Rocket" Richard Trophy was unveiled by the NHL. The trophy was given by the Canadiens as an annual award for the league's top goal-scorer as chosen by the NHL Board of Governors. Richard presented its first winner, Teemu Selanne, with it at the annual NHL awards.

And as if Richard hadn't already been immortalized: in 2005, *The Rocket*, a film based on Richard's life, was made. The film was an excellent and honest portrayal of a man who gave hope and new life to hockey fans and French-Canadians.

The Rocket is still as ubiquitous as ever. His status as a cultural icon cannot be disputed. Driving or walking through

One of the many monuments created in honour of the Rocket. This one rests in Gatineau, Quebec.

Quebec, finding a statue or painting or photo posted somewhere is an easy task. His name is found in songs and poems and, of course, countless hockey books. In 1995, thirty-five years after he last played, a Maurice Richard figurine was issued (for children four years and older). In 2004, the Canadian Museum of Civilization staged their exposition entitled, "Rocket Richard: the Legend—The Legacy." You can even find an image of The Rocket on a commemorative stamp. When Shania Twain appeared at the 2003 Juno Awards, she didn't just wear a sparkling Montreal Canadiens jersey: she wore it with Richard's number 9. Even Celine Dion performed in 1998 wearing the iconic Canadiens jersey with Richard's number. His name and number will be forever emblazoned in the Canadian consciousness.

* * *

Maurice Richard, the quiet, the strong, was able to unintentionally unite a people through a simple game.

"Neither the Catholic religion with its aspirations for the other world nor our political leaders, so absurdly small before the forces of this world, makes us shiver with pride at simply being alive the way the Rocket does," Roch Carrier once said.

Maurice Richard

Some say that Quebec's "Quiet Revolution" began with Maurice Richard. He embodied a people who'd long been marginalized. They were a rich culture fighting to be recognized as equals to the English. And Richard was no different. He joined a hockey club that was ruled by Anglophones. But he never let that stop him from doing what he did best. It was inspiring.

The Montreal *Gazette*'s Red Fisher once said, "He carried the flag for an entire population—and that's pretty heavy. He felt he had to live up to that responsibility and he did it the way he knew how—by scoring goals and responding to every challenge on the ice."

On March 11, 1996, when fans were bidding *adieu* to their cathedral, their Forum, both French-Canadians and English-Canadians stood to recognize an idol. The divisions were forgotten; the struggles left outside the doors. And after thirty-six long years, the Rocket stood again at centre ice. Richard was heavier, greyer, slower, but he still possessed those eyes that had inspired a people. And those people, Francophone and Anglophone alike, rose to their feet and applauded for eight long minutes.

"He hadn't scored a goal or played a game there in thirty-six years," Dick Irvin Jr. told *Maclean's*. "And people were crying, for God's sake. What other athlete, any place, any time, would get that kind of ovation from that kind of an audience? It showed what he meant to Quebec and to Montreal. And it wasn't just Francophones—he was a hero to Anglophones, too."

Legacy

Richard had found a way, through the country's national pastime, to cross borders and break down walls. His grit and determination was inspiring to both the French and English. He was what everyone wanted to be: talented, tough, and tenacious, unafraid to stand up to those who tried to push him down or stop him on the way to his goal. The fire in his eyes, something he was renowned for, spoke to everyone.

French-Canadians had most certainly felt persecuted, even in their pastime. Before Richard, their beloved Montreal Canadiens were hardly representative of the French in Quebec. Owned by Anglophones, played by Anglophones, their identity in even the national pastime seemed to be neglected. The goal, set so long ago by Ambrose O'Brien and Jimmy Gardner, to provide Montreal with a French team had failed. If they couldn't even fight to be represented on the ice, how could they expect to be represented throughout Canada? French-Canadians needed hope. And hope is what they received. Their saviour carried a stick, and when he took to the ice against the English teams, he made them weep.

Goalie Glenn Hall once said of Richard, "His eyes were terrifying. When he was roaring towards me with the puck, they would sparkle, crackle like a pinball machine."

It was that fire that had ignited a province.

As Richard stood at centre ice the night of March 11, 1996, Richard Garneau, the Forum announcer, exclaimed,

"He is seen as a symbol of an entire nation that recognizes itself in his exploits and in his personality."

That quiet yet fierce determination of a man who other players—mainly English—had attempted to smother, was what excited a people. Like the people of Quebec, Richard faced obstacles on the ice because he was French-Canadian. And the people saw his determination and strength on the ice as a mirror of what they were, what they could be, in a country where they were the minority. When he skated with a man on his back and scored, it was as though the French-Canadian people saw themselves succeeding despite years of oppression. Richard may not have been the most graceful player, but he was there when his team needed him. He was there when Quebec needed him.

"Before René Levesque, before Lucien Bouchard, before Robert Charlebois, he was the first symbol in a time for people, then known as French-Canadians, now known as Québécois. Maurice Richard was the symbol for the little people, the French-Canadian who went with his lunchbox to the factory of the English-Canadian," said journalist Rejean Tremblay.

The night of the Forum closing, Richard stood on the ice with other Canadiens greats like Jean Béliveau, Ken Dryden, and Guy Lafleur. Richard was overcome by the fans and the standing ovation. Three minutes into the ovation, tears came to his eyes and he rubbed at his face, clearly trying to hold back the well of emotion. He seemed uncomfortable with the outpouring of admiration from the almost 18,000 fans, most of whom had never seen him play. He was, once again, the reluctant hero. The man who thought he was "just a hockey player."

Later, Richard would say of that night, "I didn't know what to say or do. I tried to stop the crowd from clapping but they kept going just the same. It was the first time I had an ovation like that."

Maurice Richard was a symbol to French-Canadians. He was a symbol of hope, of perseverance, of triumph. He was so much more than simply a man on skates.

"We had come out of a Depression right into a World War, and people's lives were being turned upside down," Frank Selke said. "We wanted a touchstone, a guy to believe in; a unique person who could make us feel secure."

Perhaps what made him more endearing to the people of Quebec was the fact that he never played the political game. He did what he did best: Maurice Richard spoke softly and carried a big stick.

* * *

On May 30, 2000—sixty-three years after Howie Morenz lay in state in the Forum—more than 115,000 people, comprised of both Québécois and Anglophones, filed past Maurice Richard as he lay in a casket at centre ice in the Molson Centre. Richard's final battle had been lost.

When doctors first discovered Richard's abdominal cancer, the prognosis wasn't good. The tumour was inoperable and most likely wouldn't respond to therapy. On top of the cancer, Richard was suffering from Parkinson's disease and arthritis in his lower spine. But Richard wasn't one to give up the fight so easily. With the same determination that saw him fend off opposing forces on the ice, Richard fought against the natural forces that were conspiring against him. And for a while, he was able to hold them off. The cancer went into remission for two years, and he still maintained his role as ambassador for the Canadiens, attending public appearances. But then the cancer returned.

Richard succumbed to the disease on March 27. It wasn't a shock to the public. Richard's illness was well known and had become public in 1998. It was hard, after all, to hide from the ravages of such a disease. Two years earlier, a photo of Richard had run on the front page of *La Dernière Heure*. The man was gaunt, clearly fending off illness. But two months later, *La Presse* ran a story announcing that he was in remission. "The Rocket's Greatest Victory."

The outpouring of grief after his death was visible throughout the province. People sought to pay their respects from all corners. Flowers and notes were left outside his apartment on Péloquin Street. People flocked to the Forum, to the place that Richard had made so sacred to hockey fans; to the place that had inspired and given hope to French-Canadians. Others sought to show their support at the Molson Centre or the Hôtel-Dieu, where he had died.

People left notes, words of praise, thanking him for all he'd done. Illustrating how much he had appeared to the French people as a saint, a saviour, one person left a note that read: "To the Rocket, be happy, and watch over me."

Quebec Premier Lucien Bouchard offered the Richard family a state funeral, which they accepted. On May 31, a national funeral service was held for the icon of Quebec in the Notre-Dame Basilica. It was a privilege few public personalities had been privy to. It was broadcast around the country.

The funeral procession wound its way down Saint-Catherine Street, past the Forum, the scene of Richard's most blessed times and also some of his hardest-fought battles. The streets weren't filled with a quiet, as one might expect of such a procession. Instead, the people of Quebec chose to honour the man that had meant so much to a generation: they applauded.

Almost 3,000 people were allowed in the basilica, which included his oldest friends and teammates like Dickie Moore, Elmer Lach, and of course, his brother

Henri. NHL commissioner Gary Bettman, Scotty Bowman, and even young NHL stars like Luc Robitaille attended. And yes, even Richard's old rival Gordie Howe paid his respects. Prime Minister Jean Chrétien, former Prime Minister Brian Mulroney, and Premier Lucien Bouchard were also in attendance. The rest of his followers watched outside of the basilica on a large screen. It was a solemn occasion, yet one that also had Québécois bursting with pride. Richard had once again brought together so many. Hundreds of thousands of people watched as hockey's greatest legend was laid to rest.

How strange a sight it must have seemed to people outside of Canada who didn't understand how much he'd meant to Canadians, in particular the French. But thirty-three years earlier, in 1967, he was one of the first people to receive the Order of Canada, our country's highest honour. The Order states, "Established in 1967 by Her Majesty Queen Elizabeth II, the Order of Canada is the centrepiece of Canada's honours system and recognizes a lifetime of outstanding achievement, dedication to the community and service to the nation. The Order recognizes people in all sectors of Canadian society. Their contributions are varied, yet they have all enriched the lives of others and made a difference to this country."

Watching his funeral and those who gathered to pay their final respects, it was evident how much of a difference he had made. Just months before, in October, the country was on the brink of being torn apart. The Quebec Referendum of 1995 was on the minds of every Canadian. Would Quebec separate from the rest of Canada? The "No" side barely prevailed, with a 50.56 per cent vote.

That day, however, as Richard's casket slowly made its way to the front of the basilica, Federalists and Separatists sat shoulder to shoulder. English-Canadians and French-Canadians shook hands. Maurice Richard had done it again. He had brought together a deeply fractured people.

To French-Canadians, Richard was a symbol of hope. He instilled a deep pride in a people long felt to be marginalized. It isn't hyperbole to say that Maurice Richard woke up a people and made them stand tall. The Quiet Revolution became the Not-So-Quiet Revolution as the years progressed, with the Québécois demanding to be recognized as a unique society within Canada. It could be said that it all started with a quiet man with a stick who refused to give up.

To English-Canadians, Richard was what made hockey great. A quiet man in the dressing room and in his day-to-day life, he breathed fire when he took to the ice. English-Canadians also recognized his passion. And they respected it.

Ultimately, however, it is the French-Canadians who feel the most connected to Richard. He transformed their game and their people.

Camille Desroches, once a publicity director for the Canadiens, summarized Richard's importance throughout Quebec: "For French people, he was our flag. We didn't have a flag; we had Maurice Richard."

Epilogue

Perhaps the greatest tribute to Maurice Richard comes from, of all things, an animation film. *The Sweater* (1980), based on a memoir by Canadian writer Roch Carrier, is set in 1946 in a small village in Quebec. The story captures the essence of a Canada that was and is. Hockey is part of daily life in this world. It is deeply connected with childhood, family, language, culture, and even religion. The radio games bring together family and community. The rink becomes a stage, a dreamland, as the boys impersonate the Rocket in the hopes that they can escape their small town. "We all wore the same costume of Maurice Richard," says Carrier. "We all combed our hair like Maurice Richard. We laced our skates like Maurice Richard. We taped our sticks like Maurice Richard. We were ten players all wearing the uniform of the Montreal Canadiens. We all wore the same number 9 on our backs."

When his Richard jersey becomes too small, his mother orders a new one from the English company, Eaton's. When the package arrives, Carrier is horrified to see a Toronto Maple Leafs jersey inside. He complains, but his mother insists that he wear it. Now he must go to the rink with his blue and white sweater.

Carrier sits on the bench for most of the game. A player

is injured. Carrier jumps on the ice. A whistle blows. He is given a penalty because he is wearing a Maple Leafs shirt. The boy, with the fire of Richard, snaps and screams, "This is persecution!" and breaks his stick. Suddenly, a very menacing, larger than life pastor appears, and sends him to church to ask for God's forgiveness.

In the final scene, Roch prays to God to send moths to eat his Leafs sweater. Suddenly, the Rocket appears, as if from the heavens. He shakes the boy's hand as though he is letting him know that he is and will always be there for Roch, for Quebec, and for Canada.

Bibliography

Béliveau, Jean, with Chrys Goyens and Allan Turowetz. *My Life in Hockey*. Greystone Books, 1994.

Carrier, Roch. *Our Life with the Rocket: The Maurice Richard Story*. Penguin Canada, 2001.

Carrier, Roch. *The Hockey Sweater*. Tundra Books, 1984.

CBC Archives

Denault, Todd. *Jacques Plante: The Man who Changed the Face of Hockey*. McClelland & Stewart, 2009.

Dowbiggin, Bruce. *The Meaning of Puck*. Key Porter Books, 2008.

Duplacey, James and Charles Wilkins. *Forever Rivals*. Random House of Canada, 1996.

Fisher, Red. *Hockey, Heroes and Me*. McClelland & Stewart, 1994.

Foran, Charles. *Maurice Richard*. Penguin Canada, 2011.

Geoffion, Bernard and Stan Fischler. *Boom Boom: The Life and Times of Bernard Geoffrion*. McGraw-Hill Ryerson Ltd., 1997.

Gowens, Chrys and Allan Turowetz, *Lions in Winter*. Prentice-Hall, 1986.

Hunter, Douglas. *War Games*. Viking, 1996.

Irwin, Dick. *The Habs: An Oral History of the Montreal*

Canadiens, 1940-1980. McClelland & Stewart, 1991.

Jenish, D'Arcy. *The Montreal Canadiens: 100 Years of Glory.* Anchor Canada, 2009.

Lacoursiere, Jacques and Robin Philpot. *A People's History of Quebec.* Baraka Books, 2002.

Macskimming, Roy. *Gordie: A Hockey Legend.* Greystone Books, 1994.

MacInnes, Craig, ed. *Remembering the Rocket.* Stoddart, 1998.

McKinley, Michael. *Hockey: A People's History.* McClelland & Stewart, 2006.

Melançon, Benoît. *The Rocket: A Cultural History of Maurice Richard.* Greystone, 2009.

O'Brien, Andy. *Rocket Richard.* Ryerson, 1961.

Richard, Maurice and Stan Fischler. *The Flying Frenchmen.* Hawthorn Books, 1971.

Robinson, Chris. *Stole This From a Hockey Card: A Philosophy of Doug Harvey, Hockey, Identity and Booze.* Nightwood Editions, 2005

Ulmer, Michael. *Canadiens Captains.* Macmillan Canada, 1996.

Acknowledgements

Eternal appreciation for the support of Nancy Sewell and James Lorimer. They know why.

Thanks also to Kelly, Jarvis and Harry Neall, Matthew Roberts, Chris Morash, Olivia Ward, and Roch Carrier.

About the Author

Chris Robinson is an Ottawa-based animation, film, literature, and sports writer. His hockey books include *Ottawa Senators* (2004), *Great Left Wingers of Hockey's Golden Era* (2006), and the critically acclaimed *Stole This From a Hockey Card* (2005). He also wrote the screenplay for the Jutra Award and Genie Award-winning animated documentary *Lipsett Diaries*, directed by Theodore Ushev.

Photo Credits

Montreal *Gazette*: p. 13, 14, 24, 43, 77; Wikipedia: p. 17; Montreal *Star*: p. 49; *Maclean's*: p. 53, 96; Canadian Press: p. 59; Roger St-Jean: p. 69; David Bier: p. 80; Canadian Museum of Civilization: cover, p. 101; Simon Pulsifer: 110.

Index

Index